S • I • T • E • S

© 1990

FASA CORPORATION

TABLE OF CONTENTS

SPRAWL SITES

Writing
Boy F. Petersen Jr.
John Faughnan
Mike Stackpole

Development
Tom Dowd

Editorial Staff
Senior Editor
Donna Ippolito
Assistant Editor
Kent Stolt
Editorial Assistant
Geri Rebstock

Production Staff
Production Manager
Sam Lewis
Art Director
Dana Knutson
Cover Art
Steve Venters
Cover Design
Joel Biske
Color Plates
Jeff Laubenstein
Illustration
Jeff Laubenstein
Earl Geier
Jim Nelson
Maps
Jon Marcus
Layout
Tara Gallagher

Published by FASA Corporation
P.O. Box 6930 Chicago, IL 60680

INTRODUCTION

prawl Sites is an invaluable reference tool for the **Shadowrun** game universe. Gamemasters will find here an abundance of information and ideas for bringing to life the strange, wonderful, and horrifying urban Sprawl of the year 2050. The opening essay, **Life On A Limb,** sets the scene. How often might one see a Metahuman walking down the street, for instance, or how many times is the average guy likely to see a Dragon in his life?

The chapter on **Location Archetypes** presents in detail more than 30 locations in the Sprawl, from residences and restaurants to chop shops and shadow tech stores. Each location also includes notes on what kinds of other characters would likely be present on the scene, as well as a map. Gamemasters will especially appreciate this section in those emergency moments when running an adventure requires them to come up with a location unexpectedly and fast.

At the heart of the book is **Sprawl Encounters,** a section for generating random encounters, followed by core descriptions of more than 130 encounters typical of various streets and neighborhoods of the Sprawl. The gamemaster may sometimes use these verbatim, or other times may find that an encounter offers the germ of an idea for an altogether different incident. Some encounters are interconnected so that the gamemaster may interweave characters and plot threads over the course of time. Some also offer the basis for whole adventures, or even a series of adventures, that he might create for his players. Most of the encounters are open-ended enough that the gamemaster can flesh out the missing details to suit his particular **Shadow-run** group and gaming style.

Contacts And Archetypes presents eight new Archetypes and 34 new Contacts to supplement those in the **Shadowrun** basic rules. In some cases, the gamemaster should note that weapons or cyberware carried by some of the Archetypes and Contacts are drawn from the **Shadowrun** source book, **Street Samurai Catalog**.

Sprawl Law provides background on the laws and levels of law enforcement in different areas of the Sprawl. Also in this section is a list of legal offenses ranging from possession of a weapon to premeditated murder and the average fine and/or prison terms those offenses carry. Finally, the chapter on **Credsticks and IDs** explains the how and why of each, both the real and the forged kind.

Sprawl Sites is intended as much as a source of ideas as a reference. Every gamemaster and every **Shadowrun** game is unique. Elements that fit well into one campaign may be ill-suited to another. Thus will gamemasters feel free to make any and all changes necessary to make the hundreds of ideas in this book work for them and their players.

LIFE ON A LIMB

Welcome to the sprawl, chummer. Hope you enjoy your stay. If nothing else, it is an interesting place. No one ever worries about having nothing to do 'cause things have a tendency to come looking for you. Want a quick tour? No problem.

Let's start classy, shall we? Heading downtown, we find the megacorporations and their multi-floored skyscrapers. (Actually, you don't have to go downtown to see the skyscrapers. You can see them from just about anywhere within kilometers around.) The styles of the buildings range from ultra-modern black macroglass to the chrome and steel architecture popular some 50 years ago. What they all have in common, though, is class. One look at these places and you know what kind of people own them.

Most corporate skyscrapers include either a stylishly landscaped outdoor promenade area or an interior, multi-story atrium/lobby that tries hard to defy description. The most elite buildings have both. Just about anybody who doesn't look threatening can get in to see these areas. It's getting upstairs that's the problem. Most corporate employees carry detailed electronic identification cards to get past the guards into the glass elevators. No card, no ride. Unless you're expected.

Outside, you'll find that downtown is one of the safest areas to be, day or night. If you don't see any municipal law enforcement, there'll be plenty of local corporate security about—and they don't take the sly wink for an answer. Most of the megacorporation buildings have access to some form of protected entryway, through either a below-ground car park or an enclosed car port, minimizing the open-air vulnerability of the corporate executives. Naturally, the wage slaves have to buck the wind and fend for themselves.

The downtown area also boasts stores, restaurants, and nightspots catering to an exclusive clientele. Mixed in there, but definitely less visible, are places for the more common folk. Even these charge more, but that's the price of being able to walk the streets at night.

Business districts make up much of the downtown area. Generally speaking, the higher the disposable income of the customers, the larger the stores. The converse is also true, as upper-class business districts also have a high number of expensive, but small, specialty shops. Good protection also holds in the upper-class residential areas. Many residential urban and suburban areas of this type rely on private security to supplement the law enforcement services supplied by either the municipality of corporate security-contract holder. In the business/downtown area, law officers carefully scrutinize pedestrians walking the streets at night, but people on foot are not particularly unusual. Not so in the residential or suburban areas. A person walking those streets late at night is twice as likely to be hassled.

Not until you get into the middle class and poorer areas do the streets become less safe. In these areas, enforcement switches from active to reactive. Even if some joker looks like a terrorist, the local cops won't do anything until he actually blows up something or starts to wave a couple of blocks of C-4 around.

Appearance is everything. Look like a hot-blooded Samurai while walking the streets of Downtown, and you'll get hassled. Look like a 600,000-nuyen-a-year executive walking the local combat zone and you'll get stopped, but for completely different reasons. The cops will bother even the most manicured Ork walking through a ritzy residential area. And God help him if he's a Troll.

Depending on the city, Metahumans make up between 10 and 25 percent of the local population. It is common to see them walking the streets, especially in the business-oriented districts. Move into the slums and the racial makeup of the average pedestrian changes, based on the neighborhood. The poorer neighborhoods tend to be more racially segregated, which increases racial tensions along the various borders. Add to that a high crime rate and rampant gang activity.

Despite what the trideo shows depict, the average citizen of the Sprawl isn't packing 60 tons of chrome and cyberware. Cybernetic samurai are definitely out there, but odds are against running into one at the local Stuffer Shack. It is possible to find shadowrunners, however, if one knows where to look.

These days, magic, in one form or another, is moderately common. In the wealthier areas of the sprawl, it is not uncommon to see the local security mage making his rounds as part of the local security force. Security mages are common in the corporate sector, too, as are various salaried wage mages. An influx of magicians has recently entered health care in the richer areas, ever since various medical schools have begun formalized degree programs in healing magic. In the rougher areas, street-level healing magic has been common for some years.

Most security and law enforcement organizations have mage detectives on staff for cases requiring the magical touch. Though not as common as other specialized detectives, the mage detective has proven a powerful asset to these organizations, putting him high on the hit lists of street gangs and organized crime groups.

Magical critters are another matter entirely. Some of them haunt the various dark corners of the less-illustrious neighborhoods, but beyond such ghouls, ghosts, specters, and the occasional vampire or banshee, the only place to see Awakened critters is in the municipal zoo.

Yes, there are Dragons around, but outside of the trideo, the average person can count on one hand the number of real dragons he'll see in his entire life. But, as everyone knows, he's better off that way.

LOCATION ARCHETYPES

Location Archetypes are detailed descriptions of businesses, residences, and other sites typical of Seattle or any other urban sprawl. These ready-to-use physical layouts may also serve as starting points for the gamemaster's own personal creations.

Each Location Archetype includes a discussion of the size, layout, and function of the site. Also included are a map of each type and information on any special physical, electronic, or magical security measures.

Each section also includes descriptions of non-player characters likely to be working or present at the location, with references to Archetypes described in the **Shadowrun** rulebook and to new types from the **Archetypes and Contacts** chapter of this book. If the NPC Archetype is simply named, it can be used without modifications. In some cases, new skills are either added or substituted.

After the gamemaster and the players have become especially familiar with a location, it is time to modify it. Imagine having the players walk into a bank where the furniture is designed to seat only large Trolls, or into a ritzy restaurant run by a burned-out mage.

BANK

SMALL BANK

Upon entering a small bank, a character notices ten to twelve computerized teller machines along the right and left walls. A technician and guard are seated at a desk in the rear. Beyond the technician and guard is a small walk-in vault holding 60 safe deposit boxes. Such a small bank is typically found in a shopping mall, in the corner of another type of store, or at a bus stop or rail station. Some small banks will rent out safety deposit boxes on an hourly basis (5¥ per hour). Blighted urban areas such as the Barrens in the Seattle Sprawl have only small banks because of the neighborhood's high crime rate.

In a typical small bank, an aisle runs between the automated tellers toward the desk where sit the technician and guard. Behind the technician is the vault door, which is only about one meter wide and deep. To the left of the vault, hidden by a panel, are the controls to the automated tellers and vault doors.

Computer

Orange-2+, Scramble 3. The computer and the automated tellers of small banks tend to be little more than large SPU slaves to the computers of the larger banks. Important information, such as the SIN numbers and financial records of those who made transactions during the day, is kept in the more secure datastores of the larger banks. The bank's most protected datastores hold the names of the day's customers and information about the safe deposit boxes. If the bank vault contains a particularly valuable item (such as an expensive piece of jewelry), or if the bank wants to prevent an information leak on a particularly important vault-user, the bank technician will download Gray IC to stand watch over the information. Banks that have been robbed of information more than once usually raise their security rating one or two levels or have a bush league decker riding herd for a time.

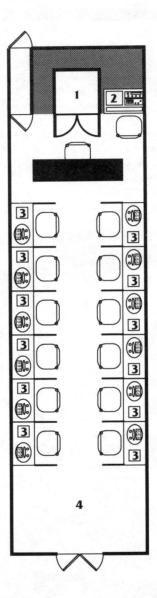

Small Bank

1. **Safe**
2. **Main Computer**
3. **Auto-Tellers**
4. **Waiting Area**

|——————|
2 Meters

Medium Bank

1.5 Meters

1. Vault
2. Computer
3. Guard Room
4. Auto-Tellers

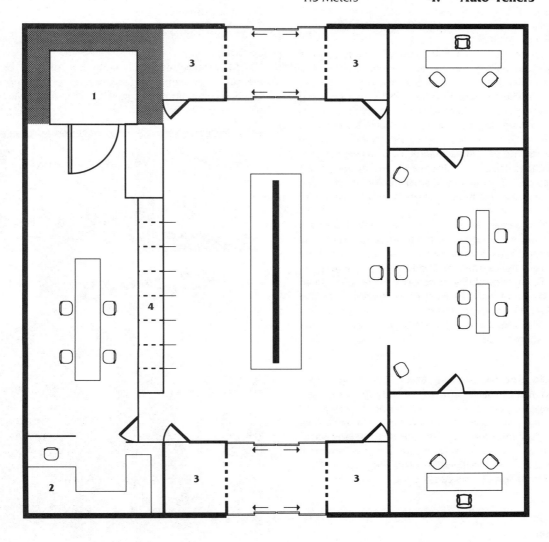

MEDIUM BANK

Medium banks serve customers with more complex financial needs, such as stock market or real estate. Customers enter the foyer of a medium bank through two sets of sliding doors. A guard observes through one-way impact glass and a metal detector carries out routine searches. The guard can lock the doors to detain suspicious customers for a more extensive search.

A medium bank is usually located on the ground floor of a large business building, with one entrance on the street and the other in the lobby. Banks built in the central city sometimes have drive-through windows. Along one side are six to ten teller machines for general banking purposes. In a corner, behind the machines, is a vault with 100 safe deposit boxes of various sizes.

On the other side of the bank are a half-dozen desks and chairs, where customers and bank officials confer on specific or general banking questions. To the rear of this area are the offices of the bank president and vice president.

Few banks allow SINless individuals to open accounts. Some banks, however, are happy to accept anyone's money, even if ill-gotten. A fixer can usually recommend this type of more "flexible" institution to a character.

Computer

Orange-5+, Blaster 3. The datastores of a medium bank contain the SIN numbers and financial records of regular customers, lists of items kept in the bank's safe deposit boxes (required in case the bank is robbed so that renters can collect the insurance), and files on the bank's staff. If a bank's computer is repeatedly hit, it usually hires an experienced minor-league decker or beefs up security with stronger IC (including Black IC if the situation warrants).

LARGE BANK

A large bank and the extra services it provides are usually the province of the rich and are often located in luxury suburban areas. They are always architecturally impressive, with scrupulously manicured landscaping, well-kept parking lots, and at least two patrol guards who are quick to question and roust anyone suspicious.

The interior of a large bank is equally impressive. It is furnished with rare woods and metals, tasteful paintings or murals decorate the walls, and employees are as beautiful as the bank. Even the lowliest tellers wear suits and dresses costing several hundred nuyen, while bank guards wear uniforms giving the impression of both elegant servility and reassuring menace.

At least four offices are devoted to extra services for the wealthiest clients. There is a stock market room, where customers sit and watch the daily activity in several stock exchanges on a large trid screen. Two adjacent stock broker offices take customer orders and offer advice. The bank also has a real estate office.

Protection for valuables kept in the large vault and the lives of the bank's many important people is top-notch. Besides the usual array of trid cameras and passive metal detectors, there are ambient veracity examiners. Though still experimental, AVEs show a remarkable ability to detect unusual stress in an individual's voice and walk. At least three guards patrol the bank on foot at all times, in addition to the guards at the entrance. Access to the bank is through security foyers similar to those of medium banks.

Computer

Private LTG, Red-5+, possibly Black IC. A large bank's datastores contain financial information on the city's wealthiest and most powerful people, as well as corporate secrets. To protect these vital stores, a corporation will give a large bank its own high-security computer. Minor-league deckers stand watch over the system around the clock. Computer contacts with small and medium banks are confined to strict timetables. Only contacts with other large banks can occur continuously.

Archetypes

Bank President

Large Bank: Use **Corporate Official**. Add Etiquette (Corporate) 4 and Special Skills of Finance (Personal) 5 and Finance (Corporate) 6.

NOTE: Small banks do not have bank presidents.

Staff

Tellers: Use **Corporate Secretary**, p. 165, **SR**. Add Interrogation 1 and Special Skill of Finance (Personal) 1.

Bank Official: Use **Corporate Official**. Add Special Skill of Finance (Personal) 2.

Bank Decker (Large banks only): Use **Corporate Decker**, p. 106, this book.

Bank Guard: Use **Corporate Security Guard**, p. 165, **SR**.

Bank Technician: Use **Technician**, p. 120, this book.

Typical Customer

Small Bank: Anyone with a bank account might be in a small bank.

Large Bank: Individuals with upper-class incomes, along with their bodyguards.

Number Of People Present

Small Bank: 1 Bank Technician, 1 Guard, 1D6 – 2 customers.

Large Bank: 1 President, 1 Vice President, 1D6 + 2 Bank Officials, 2 Brokers, 1 Real Estate Agent, 1 Bank Decker, 1D6 + 2 Guards, 3D6 + 2 Customers.

Security

Most bank security is limited to physical or electronic measures, but some large banks, especially those in more luxurious neighborhoods, may have a contract with a firm supplying magical security.

Large Bank

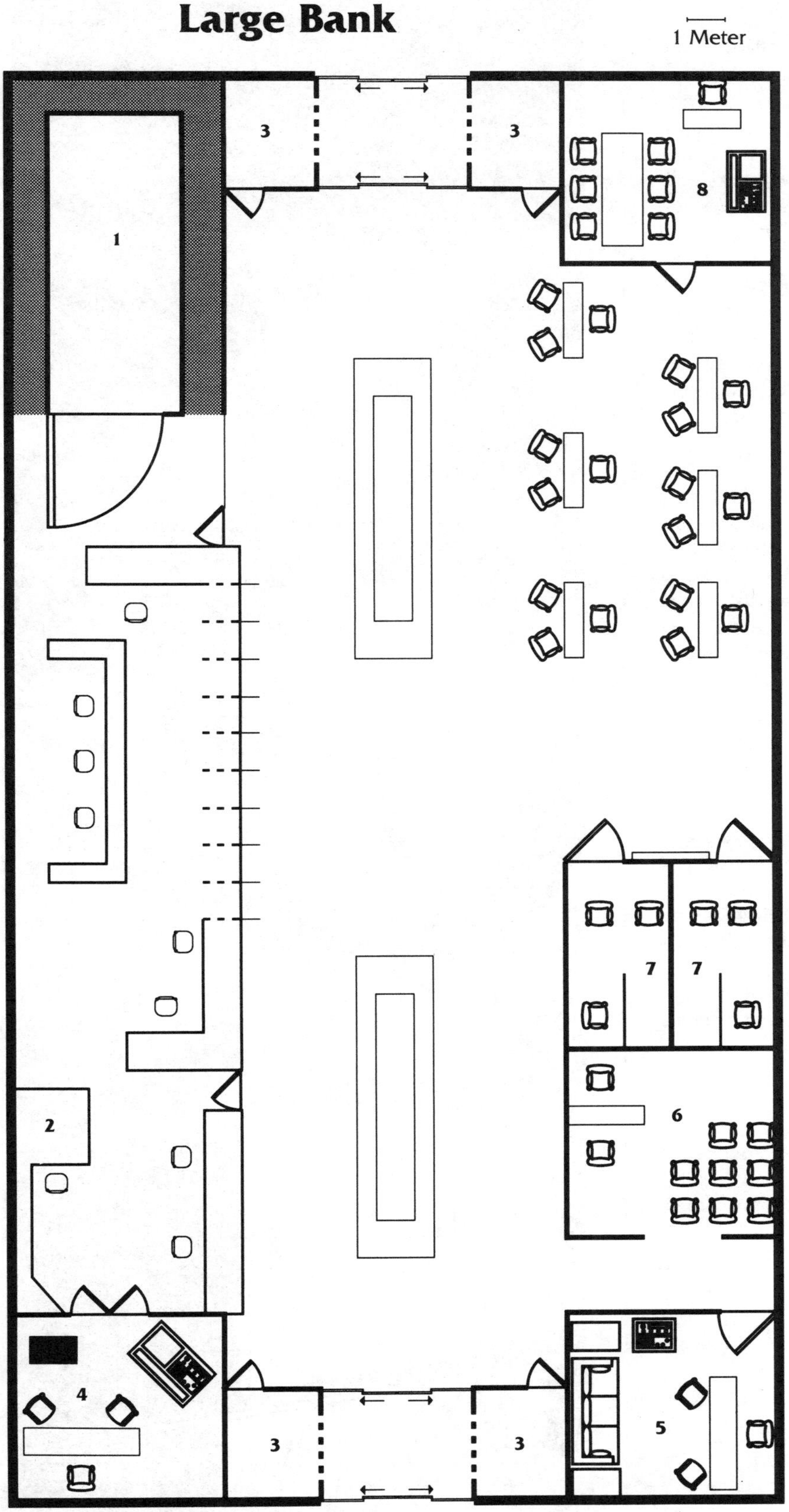

1 Meter

1. Vault
2. Computer
3. Guard Room
4. V.P. Office
5. President's Office
6. Stock Watcher's Room
7. Brokers' Office
8. Real Estate Agent's Office

BAR

Most bars are small (12m x 26m) with room for the bar, four booths, four small tables, and a small stage. Alongside the coat rack at the door are stairs leading up to a restaurant or down to a storeroom. The bar counter extends almost the entire length of the room, curving in at one end. Behind the bar is a large, two-way mirror that allows the owner or bouncer to watch from the storeroom and office. In respectable bars, tables and chairs are constructed of finer materials. Seedy bars use chipped and disfigured monstrosities of plastic and metal.

The more respectable bars are well-lit, happy places filled with good cheer and laughter. In the smoky darkness of less respectable bars, the music is muted and the people often menacingly silent. Bartenders in such seedy bars can often help customers make contact with people able to satisfy any vice. The bartender makes no judgments, having seen it all.

Computer

Green-4, Scramble 1. Most bars have little need for a powerful computer hooked up to the LTG. Small personal computers can handle records of their inventory and finances. If the bar is part of a chain, a larger, more secure computer is used to allow for communications between establishments. Seedy bars are unlikely to have any computer. Exceptions are those that front for the mob, often equipped with large and powerful systems to keep track of their many illegal activities.

Archetypes

Bar Owner: Use **Bartender**, p. 163, **SR**. Etiquette (Corporate) 1, and Negotiation 2.

Bartender: Use **Bartender**.

Staff: Use **Squatter**, p. 170, **SR**. Increase Charisma to 3, and add Etiquette (Street) 3, Unarmed Combat 1, and Special Skill of Street Rumormill 3.

Bar Bouncer: Respectable bars hire a **Troll Bouncer**, p. 173, **SR**. Seedier bars will hire any big brute. Use **Company Man**, p. 164, **SR**, but with only combat skills.

Respectable Bar Customer: Anyone with a high enough income. The bouncer makes short work of anyone who seems out of place.

Seedy Bar Customer: Anyone.

Number Of People Present

Respectable Bar: 1 Owner, 1 Bartender, 1 Bouncer, 2 Waitstaff, 3D6 Customers.

Seedy Bar: 1 Owner, 1 Bartender, 1 Waitstaff, 2D6 Customers.

Bar

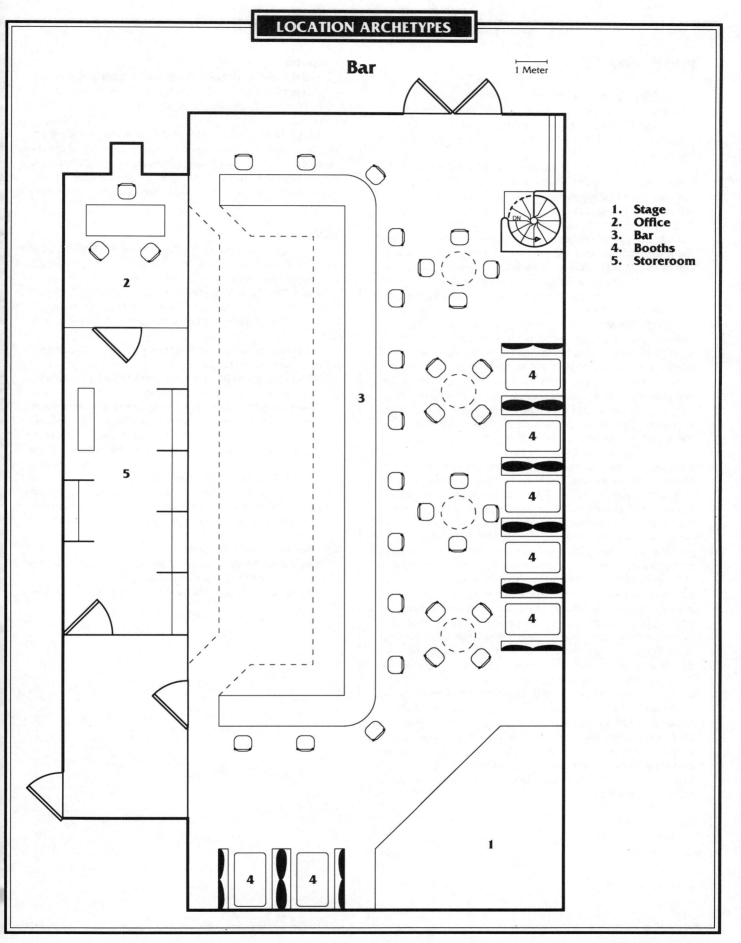

1 Meter

1. Stage
2. Office
3. Bar
4. Booths
5. Storeroom

BODY SHOP

"Replacing meat with machine" is a crude but concise description of what goes on in a body shop. Depending on how much nuyen someone wants to spend, a body shop can offer everything from a simple chipjack implant to a complete limb replacement.

Legal body shops, those accredited by the city and the CAMA (Canadian-American Medical Association), usually operate as part of the services offered by hospitals. At these body shops (often called "Physical Enhancement Clinics" by image-conscious hospitals), the customer can be sure of obtaining top-quality cyberware and vat-grown replacements. The client also knows that experts are standing by in case of emergency. Every cyberware implant comes with extensive training sessions, service contracts, and long guarantees. Many legal body shops employ staff healers to perform magical cures on patients. These services, naturally, cost extra.

Illegal body shops are another matter. Someone who wants a cyberware implant but no publicity will turn to an illegal shop (known on the streets as a chop shop or butchery). Most illegal shops are located in the back rooms of doctors' and dentists' offices, while electronics stores, sporting goods stores, and even candy stores may also serve as fronts. An illegal body shop offers guarantees for neither the operation nor the parts, so payment is in advance. Many patients have drifted off under the anesthetic, only to be discarded with the next morning's trash. The cyberware in an illegal shop is usually of local manufacture and of poor quality. A street doc occasionally has first-rate cyberware, but it probably stinks of murder and the police. Those who survive a chop-shop procedure will receive an instruction chip or manual on the cyberware, then be hustled back out onto the street, where the individual will have to fathom the workings of his new body part by himself.

The typical body shop is about 18m by 28m. The front 6m x 18m in a legal shop or clinic is a reception area where patients check in and family and friends wait. In an illegal shop, this area serves as the shop's cover, operating as some other kind of business. Beyond the reception area are the examination room and doctor's office. Because of the great demand for implanted cyberware, the operating theaters, usually two per clinic, are rather small by hospital standards, with just enough room for a doctor and two nurses. Equipment, such as anesthesia and diagnostic tools, is built into the wall and floors. Machinery under the operating table can be raised to enclose the body and submerge it in nutrient fluids for operations involving the implantation of vat-grown organ replacements. In a legal body shop, the doctor can use a wall intercom to contact other surgeons or doctors in case of complications. At the rear of the operating theater is the scrub room, where the cyberware is kept in refrigerated lockers and hooked up to diagnostic equipment until needed.

Computer

Legal Shop: Orange-2, Trace and Report 3. If the body shop is part of a hospital, the computer CPU is downgraded to an SPU. Records of the shop's most recent patients are heavily protected.

Illegal Shop: Red-3, Trace and Burn 4. Illegal body shops and their customers are more than a little paranoid about the possible theft of information about their activities and identities, respectively. If a major underworld gang owns the shop, a minor-league decker may be watching over the shop's computer system.

Archetypes

Legal Shop Surgeon: Use **Street Doc**, p. 171, **SR**. Add Etiquette (Corporate) 3, Etiquette (Street) 1, and Psychology 2.

Illegal Shop Surgeon: Use **Street Doc**.

Legal Shop Nurse: Use **Street Doc**. Add Biology 2, Biotech 4, Etiquette (Corporate) 2, Etiquette (Street) 2, Psychology 1.

Legal Shop Guard: Use **Corporate Security Guard**, p. 165, **SR**.

Illegal Shop Nurse: Use **Street Doc**. Biological Sciences 1, Biotech 3, and Etiquette (Street) 3.

Illegal Shop Guard: Use **Corporate Security Guard**. Etiquette (Street) 4, Firearms 4, and Unarmed Combat 4.

Legal Shop Customer: Legal shops service more prosperous folk interested in appearance-enchancing cyberware, such as stylishly pointed ears or neon-rimmed irises. Corporate deckers and bodyguards come in for performance-enhancing cyberware implants.

Illegal Shop Customer: Typical customers include someone running from the law who wants cosmetic surgery to change his appearance, or someone wanting performance enhancement without the need of informing the authorities.

Number Of People Present

Legal Body Shop: 1 Doctor, 2 Nurses, 1 Receptionist, 1 or 2 Patients, 1–4 Family Members, 1 Guard.

Illegal Body Shop: 1 Doctor, 1 Nurse, 1 Patient, 2 Guards.

Body Shop/Clinic

1 Meter

1. **Reception Area**
2. **Examination/Recovery Room**
3. **Doctors' Office**
4. **Operating Theaters**
5. **Scrub Room & Cyberware Room**
6. **Medical Instrument & Drug Room**

BUS STATION

The average bus terminal is 20m x 38m long with the two bus lanes splitting the station in half. People enter the station via four flights of stairs, two escalators, and four elevators. Small kiosks and pushcart salesmen cluster around the stairs and elevators. On corners near the bus roads are rooms where conductors keep watch over the crowd, raising and lowering the safety barriers when buses come and go. When no buses are in the station, conductors raise safety rails across the road to permit passage on foot.

Vagrants and transients like to hang out in bus stations, especially during evening and late hours. The homeless also seek its warmth, especially during the cold winter months.

Computer

Orange-3, Trace-4. Not much need for tight security here. Staff records and schedules are not usually considered inside information.

Archetypes

Conductor: Use **Corporate Security Guard**, p. 165, **SR**. Electronics (Safety Rail Mechanism) 1.

Guard: Use **Corporate Security Guard**, with Troll modifiers.

Customer: Anyone with a middle-class lifestyle might be found in the bus station during daylight hours. At night, the number of Humans and Elves drops dramatically. Many Orks and Trolls are in the station at all hours.

Number Of People Present

Daytime: 2 Conductors, 2 Guards, 6 Pushcart Salesmen, and 1D6 x 5 Passengers.

Evening: 2 Conductors, 4 Guards, 3 Pushcart Salesmen, and 3D6 Passengers.

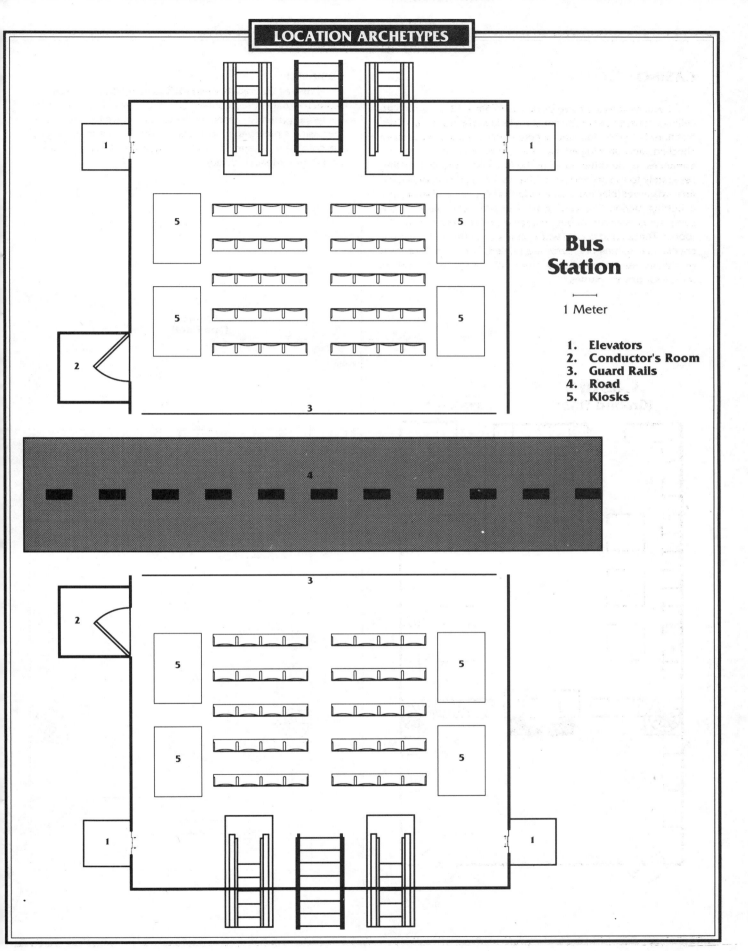

Bus Station

— 1 Meter

1. **Elevators**
2. **Conductor's Room**
3. **Guard Rails**
4. **Road**
5. **Kiosks**

CASINO

Local casinos are three stories tall, 75m x 120m, with high ceilings constructed of the finest materials. The front half of the first floor is a reception area, where patrons' hats and coats are checked, and an elegant bar. On either side of the bar are entrances to the other areas of the first floor, and stairs rising separately to the second floor. The rest of the first floor is used for card games (blackjack, various forms of poker, and so on) and a betting parlor. The card games usually take place in the sumptuous main room, but private parties can rent out smaller rooms. The second floor is where craps, roulette, and the more spectacular games of chance are played. The third floor is an expensive restaurant offering a vista of the Sprawl as well as rooms for private parties.

Computer

Private LTG, Red-8, Killer-4, Trace and Burn. The casino's protected datastores contain SIN and credit information on everyone currently present in the casino, as well as records on the casino's preferred customers. To ensure customer privacy, the computer is large and well-defended by IC and an experienced minor-league decker.

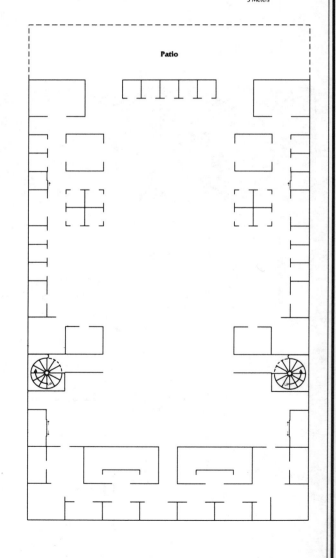

Casino
(2nd Floor)

5 Meters

Casino
(Ground Floor)

2.5 Meters

Archetypes

Casino Owner: Use **Club Owner**, p. 106, this book.

Hosts and Hostesses: Use **Corporate Secretary**, p. 165, **SR**, with Charisma 6, Etiquette (Corporate) 2, Etiquette (Media) 2, Etiquette (Street) 2 Interrogation 1, Negotiation 2, Psychology 3.

Game Staffers: Use **Corporate Secretary**, with Charisma 5, Etiquette (Corporate) 1, Etiquette (Media) 1, Etiquette (Street) 1, and Game Skill (Specialization in one game) 4.

Guard: Use **Corporate Security Guard**, p. 165, **SR**.

Typical Patron: Anyone who can afford an upper or luxury class lifestyle.

Number Of People Present

1 Casino Owner, 20 Hosts, 50 Game Staffers, 20 Guards, 2D6 x 10 Customers.

Security

Magical security is as important as physical and electronic security for casinos. Though the places may not be able to afford a staff security mage, they frequently hire one for special events or if a steady customer continues to win big.

Casino
(Top Floor)

5 Meters

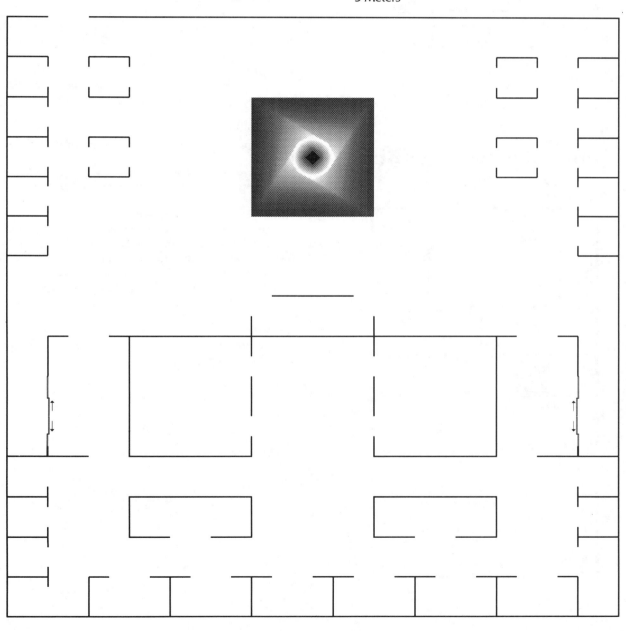

CORPORATE OFFICE

SMALL OFFICE

A small office is 3m x 4m, with just enough room for a desk, three chairs, a computer, and some shelves.

JUNIOR EXECUTIVE OFFICE

A junior executive office is 6m x 10m. A 6m x 4m. reception area includes the secretary's desk, several chairs, and a couch. The executive office contains a large desk, small couch, and plenty of shelf space.

SENIOR EXECUTIVE SUITE

The senior executive suite is 20m x 18m. The reception area has one receiving desk, two work desks, chairs, and a sofa. The executive office has one large desk, a table and chairs, a couch, a bar, and numerous shelves. The spare room, hidden behind a secret door, is often used as a private conference room or bedroom. The room is 6m x 6m, with bath attached.

Computer

Executive computers vary according to the corporation. They normally tie into the larger corporate system.

Archetypes

Corporate Executive: Use **Corporate Official**, p. 107, this book.

Secretary: Use **Corporate Secretary**, p. 165, **SR**.

Guard: Use **Corporate Security Guard**, p. 165, **SR**.

Number Of People Present

Small Office: 1 Corporate Official, maybe with guest.

Junior Executive Offices: 1 Corporate Official, 1 Corporate Secretary, and 1 visiting Corporate Official.

Senior Executive Suite: 1 Corporate Official, 2 Corporate Secretaries, 1 Corporate Guard. Visiting are 1 Corporate Official, 1 Corporate Guard.

Security

Corporate offices usually rely on equal parts of physical, electronic, and magical security.

Small Corporate Office

1 Meter

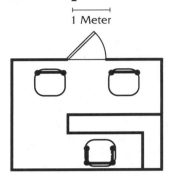

Junior Executive Office

1 Meter

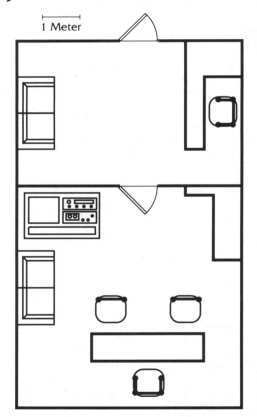

Senior Executive Office

1 Meter

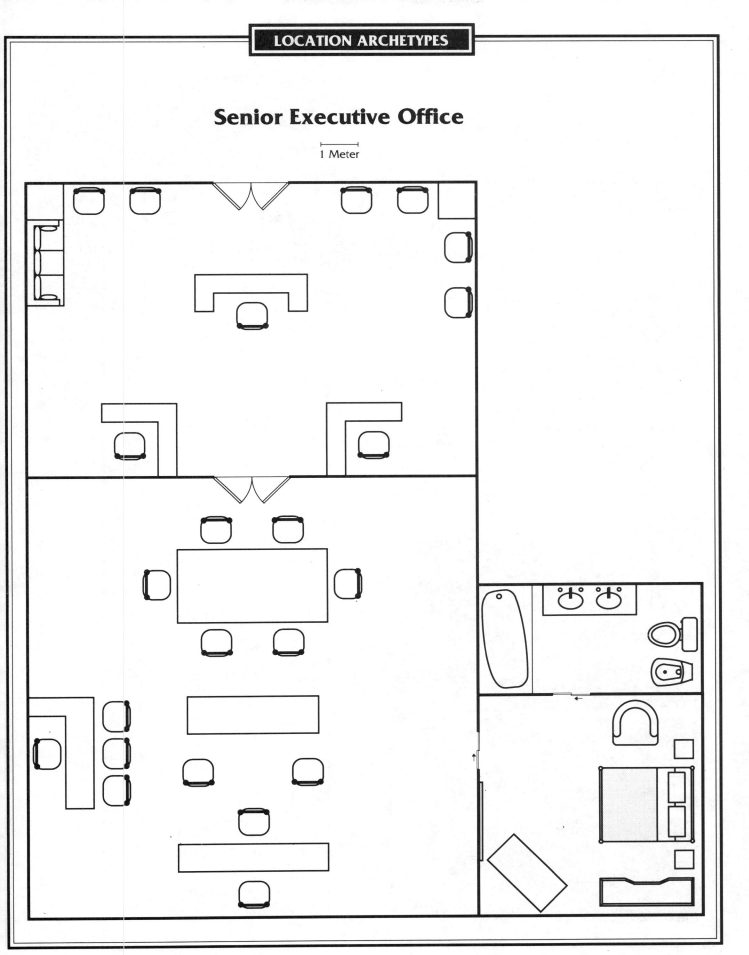

DOCK

The average dock is 30m wide by 100 meters long. Docks are built from steel, though a few wooden ones still exist. A warehouse stretches most of the dock's length, with five doors able to open to a width of ten meters (two doors on each side and one at the end). At the end of the dock are two mobile hammerhead cranes able to lift ten tons of freight.

Computer

Green-5, Barrier 3. The dock computer system contains ship manifests, schedules, warehouse inventory, and the cargo. Information is routinely transferred to the main office computer.

Archetypes

Dock Boss: Use **Corporate Security Guard**, p. 165, **SR**, with Etiquette (Corporate) 1, Etiquette (Street) 4, Firearms 2, Intelligence 3, Unarmed Combat 4.

Crane Operator: Use **Squatter**, p. 170, **SR**, with Etiquette (Corporate) 2, Etiquette (Street) 3, Firearms 2, Helo Crane Operation 4, Mobile Crane Operation 4.

Longshoreman: Use **Company Man**, p. 164, **SR**, with only Combat Skills. Add Etiquette (Street) 2.

Number Of People Present

1 Dock Boss, 2 Crane Operators, 2D6 x 4 Longshoremen, 3 Guards.

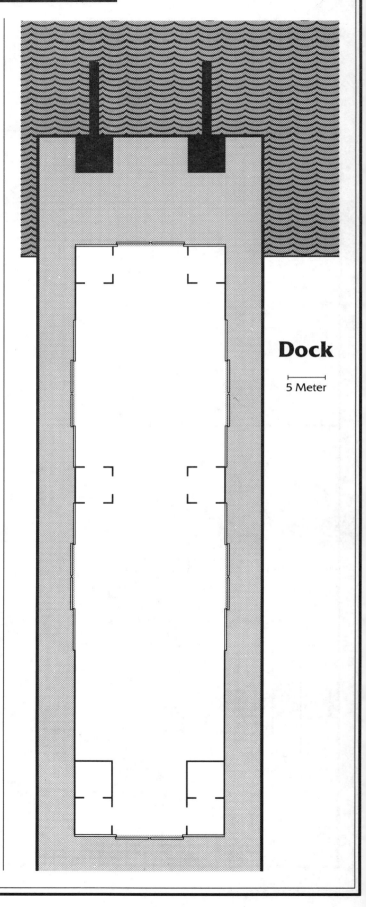

Dock

5 Meter

Fire Station

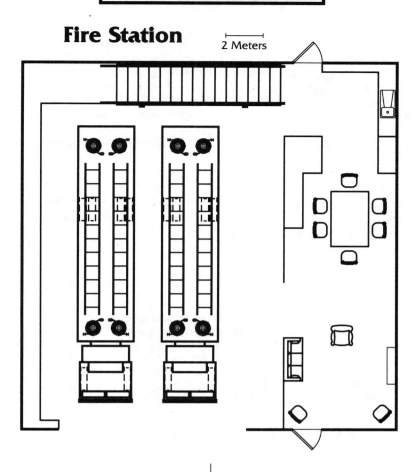

2 Meters

FIRE STATION

A typical fire station consists of a garage area for parking fire vehicles, a kitchen, and a sleeping area. The garage is at least 20m x 14m to accommodate the two large fire vehicles. At the rear are lockers and stairs leading to the second-floor sleeping area. Next to the garage is the kitchen/living area, where the firemen lounge, eat, and wait until a call comes. On the roof is a helicopter able to carry men and their equipment, as well as an arsenal of firefighting equipment.

Computer

Orange-3, Trace and Dump 3. Mischief-makers delight in causing false alarms. To prevent this, most fire-fighting corporations take pains to make their computers as secure as possible.

Archetypes

Fire Chief: Use **Fire Fighter**, p. 111, this book. Add Biotech 2, Computer 3, Etiquette (Corporate) 3, Etiquette (Street) 2, Fire-Fighting Skills 6, Leadership 2.

Fire Fighters: Use **Fire Fighter**.

Number Of People Present

1 Fire Chief, 7 Fire Fighters, 2 Riggers, 2 Corporate Guards.

HOSPITAL

The typical hospital is a multi-storied building (at least three floors), with specialized wards and laboratories on each floor. The main floor of a small hospital is 200m x 50m. The nurses' station is centrally located in a wide main corridor. Near the nurses' station are elevators. The wings of the hospital have labs, operating rooms, and patients' rooms. All rooms are connected via a computer and intercom system.

Computer

Red-3, Trace and Report 5. Because lives depend on the speed and reliability of the hospital's computer, administrators go to great lengths to ensure that no one interferes with the system. At least one minor-league decker is on call to help defend the system.

Archetypes

Hospital Chief Administrator: Use **Corporate Official**, p. 107, this book. Add Biology 3, Biotech 3, and Special Skill of Hospital Administration 5.

Doctors: Use **Street Doc**, p. 171, **SR**. Add Etiquette (Corporate) 3, Etiquette (Street) 1, Negotiation 4, Psychology 2.

Nurse: Use **Street Doc**, with Biology 4, Biotech 4, Etiquette (Corporate) 2, Etiquette (Street) 2, Psychology 1.

Guard: Use **Corporate Security Guard**, p. 165, **SR**.

Number Of People Present

1 Chief Hospital Administrator, 20 Hospital Administrators, 50 Doctors, 200 Nurses, 50 Guards, 2D6 x 20 patients.

Hospital

2 Meters

1. **Double Bed Rooms**
2. **Single Bed Rooms**
3. **Cyberware Prep Room**
4. **Cyberware Storage**
5. **Operating Theater**
6. **Scrub Room**
7. **Pharmacy**
8. **Nurse Station**

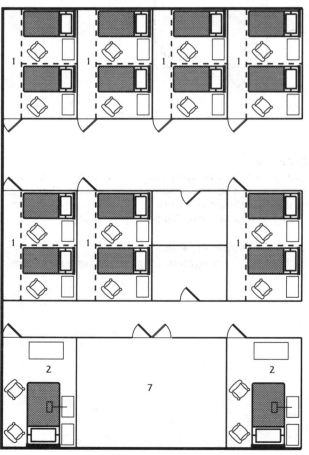

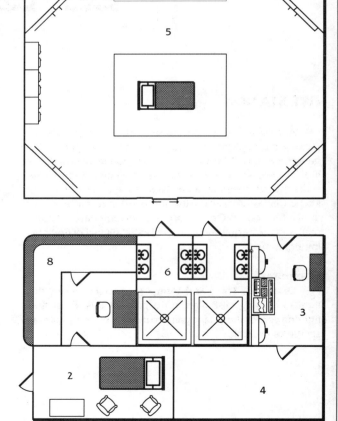

HOTEL

CHEAP HOTEL

Most cheap hotels use variations on the stackable plastic cubicles made popular by the Japanese in the late 20th century. A 1m x 1m x 2m cubicle usually contains a small flat-screen television, clock radio, air conditioning, and a thin mattress. There are separate shower rooms, luggage lockers, datanet access via several pay telecom sets, and a small kitchen with plenty of nuke foodstuffs for sale. Most of these "Coffin Hotels," as they are sometimes known, line up the cubicles in long rows and stack them four (sometimes even five) high to use every bit of space.

Though most cheap hotels are respectable, a number have become the haven of the city's worst types.

Computer

Green-3, Scramble 3. As guest lists are the most important bit of information stored in a hotel's computer, but so few people give their real names in a cheap hotel, theft of computer data is simply not a problem.

Cheap Hotel

1 Meter

1. **Kitchen**
2. **Washroom**
3. **Laundry**
4. **Showers**
5. **Front Desk**

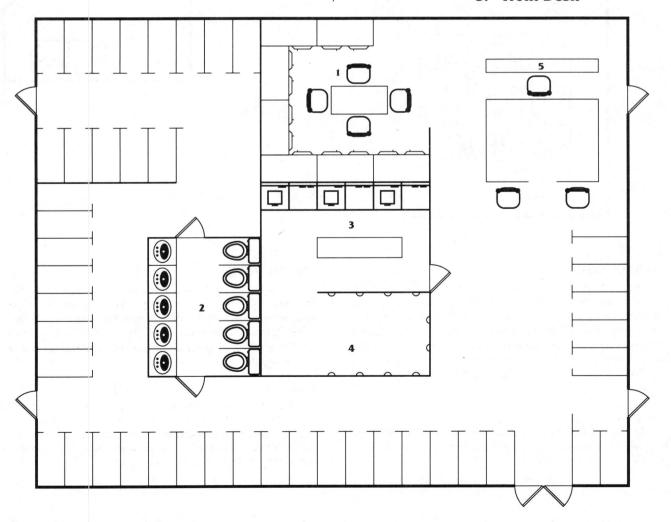

Average Hotel

|— 2 Meter —|

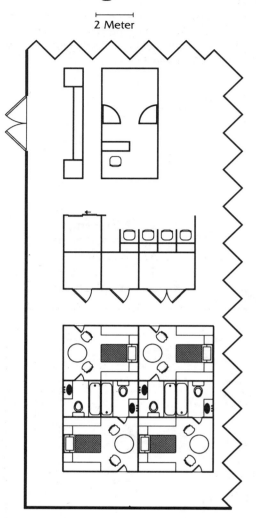

Luxury Hotel Room

|— 1 Meter —|

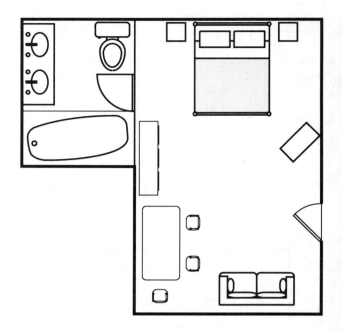

AVERAGE HOTEL

An average hotel generally offers one comfortable room (4m x 3m) with a bed, a table and chairs, a small trideo set, and bathroom with a small tub. Some hotels permit automatic check-in by slotting a credstick into a machine. After deducting the room cost from the person's credstick, the machine assigns the customer a room number; the credstick becomes the room key. Some larger hotel chains have small restaurants and room service.

Computer

Orange-4, Blaster 3. Average hotels take a little more care to protect computer files because the hotel guests are less likely to conceal their identities.

LUXURY HOTEL

A luxury hotel offers a guest at least one large room (8m x 5m) with a full-size bathroom. Larger suites have many rooms, each with its own elaborate entertainment system and computer. Luxury hotels have huge (20m x 20m), often ornate, lobbies where guests register and uniformed bell hops assist with baggage.

Computer

Red-6, Trace and Dump 4. The guests are usually so rich and famous that they try to remain inconspicuous while traveling. The luxury hotel's computer must be able to defend its guests' identities to the bitter end. Many luxury hotels employ minor-league deckers to monitor their files.

Luxury Hotel
(Section of Lobby)

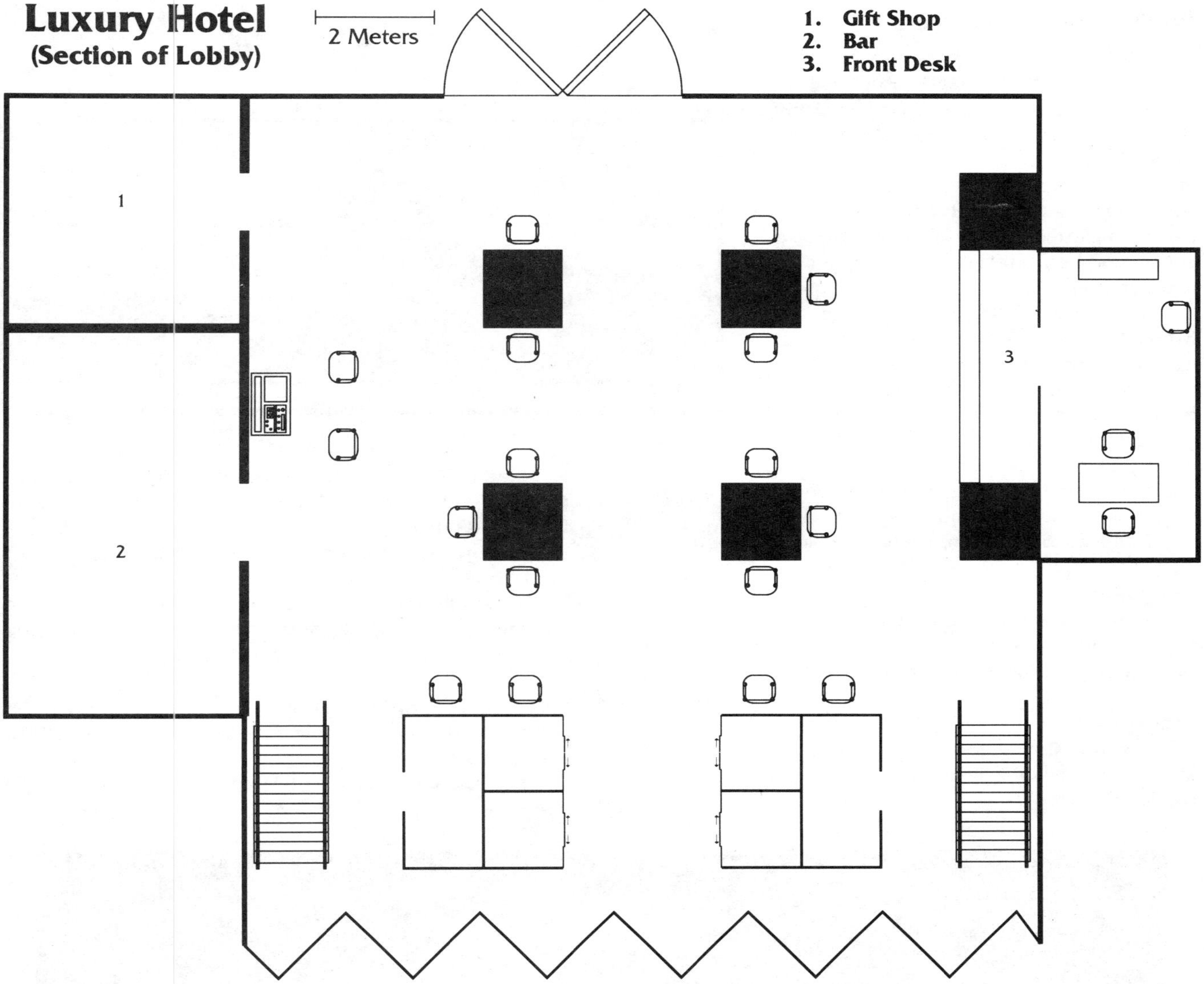

2 Meters

1. Gift Shop
2. Bar
3. Front Desk

Archetypes

Cheap Hotel Manager: Use **Bartender**, p. 163, **SR**, with Etiquette (Street) 4, Firearms 2, Unarmed Combat 2, and Special Skill of Hotel Management 3.

Average and Luxury Hotel Manager: Use **Corporate Official**, p. 107, this book. (Ratings in parentheses are luxury hotel managers.) Etiquette (Corporate) 3 (4), Etiquette (Media) 1 (3), Negotiation 2 (3), and Special Skill of Hotel Management 3 (5).

Maids or Bellhops: Use **Corporate Secretary**, p. 165, **SR**, as follows. First numbers are for workers at small hotels, numbers in parentheses are for middle class and luxury hotel staffs, respectively. Computer 1, (1)/(2), Etiquette (Corporate) 0, (1)/(3), Etiquette (Media) 1, (2)/(3), Etiquette (Street) 3, (2)/(2), Hotel Skills 1, (2)/(2), Being Ignored 6, (6)/(5), Hotel Rumormill 2, (4)/(6).

Guards: Use **Corporate Security Guard**, p. 165, **SR**, with no modifications.

Cheap Hotel Guests: Anyone up to middle class.

Average Hotel Guests: People with middle-class lifestyles.

Luxury Class Hotel Guests: People with luxury lifestyles.

Number Of People Present

Cheap Hotels: 1 Owner, 2 Staff, 3 Guards, 2D6 x 10 Guests.

Average Hotel: 1 Owner, 20 Staff, 8 Guards, 1D6+2 x 10 Guests.

Luxury Class Hotel: 1 Owner, 60 Staff, 30 Guards, 2D6 x 10 Guests.

Security

Only luxury class hotels can afford magical security, and they buy it heavily.

MONORAIL STATION

To reach the typical monorail station, passengers take protected stairs rising over the street and leading to the monorail's concrete support just below the tracks. There, passengers touch their credsticks to turnstiles, which issue them tickets and let them through. To continue up to the station, passengers may take either the stairs or one of the two elevators built into a concrete pillar.

The station is 120m x 40m, and set between the two monorail tracks. It is covered, usually well-lit, and relatively clean. Guard rails and gates keep people well away from the tracks. When a train pulls into the station, the gate and ramp mechanisms extend to the doors of the station and are in place before the train doors open. Most stations have an assortment of magazine stands, snack food bars, and shoe shine stands.

Some monorail stations are built within buildings.

Computer

Red-2 Trace 4. The local transit authority guards its computer heavily because so many lives depend on its ability to safely coordinate the monorails.

Archetypes

Monorail Conductor: Use **Corporate Secretary,** p. 165, **SR**, with Computer 3, Electronics 2, Etiquette (Corporate) 2, Etiquette (Street) 1.

Monorail Station

10 Meters

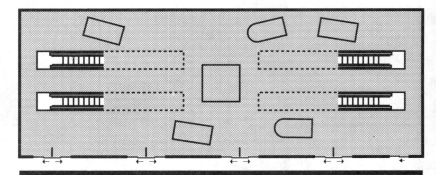

Station Mechanic: Use **Mechanic**, p. 168, **SR**, with Computer 3, Computer Theory 4, Electronics 3, Electronics (B/R) 4, Etiquette (Corporate) 1, Ground Vehicles (B/R) 5.

Station Guard: Use **Corporate Security Guard**, p. 165, **SR** rules.

Typical Rider: Middle-class wage slaves or tourists looking for a scenic view of the city. At night, the monorail is considered the safe alternative to the streets and the bus terminal.

Number Of People Present

Not In Station: 1 Conductor, 1 Mechanic, 4 Guards, 2D6 x 2 Passengers.

In Station: 1 Conductor, 1 Mechanic, 4 Guards, 1D6 x 10 Passengers.

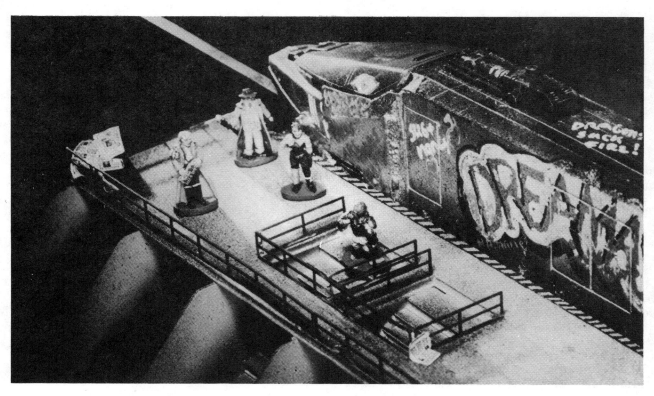

NIGHT CLUB

The typical night club is a 50m x 30m building. A space 18m x 30m is devoted to rooms for performers and for storage of stage gear behind the stage and curtain. The 14m x 30m space immediately in front of the 10m x 10m stage contains booths along the walls and an open area for dancing or observing. Up a short flight of stairs from the dance floor are the bar and more booths and tables. The owner's office is usually behind the bar.

Computer

Orange-5, Killer 3. The shadier club owners keep far too many people's names and embarrassing personal details about them in their computers to leave them unprotected.

Archetypes

Night-Club Owner: Use **Club Owner**, p. 106, this book.
Wait Staff: Use **Corporate Secretary**, p. 165, **SR**, with Etiquette (Street) 4, Unarmed Combat 2, and Special Skills of Street Rumormill 2 and Media Rumormill 2.
Bouncer: Use **Troll Bouncer**, p. 173, **SR**.
Typical Customer: Young men and women with a passion for the particular static the club passes off as music. Sometimes clubs instruct bouncers to turn away all but the most "beautiful people." That means discrimination, not only against those who do not meet some beauty standard, but against other races. For the average patron, use the **Club Habitué**, p. 104, this book.

Number Of People Present

1 Owner, 2 Bartenders, 6 Waitstaff, 3 Bouncers, 1D6 x 6 Customers.

Night Club

1 Meter

1. Bar
2. Office
3. Store Room
4. Booth
5. Stage
6. Dressing Room
7. Restroom
8. Meeting Room

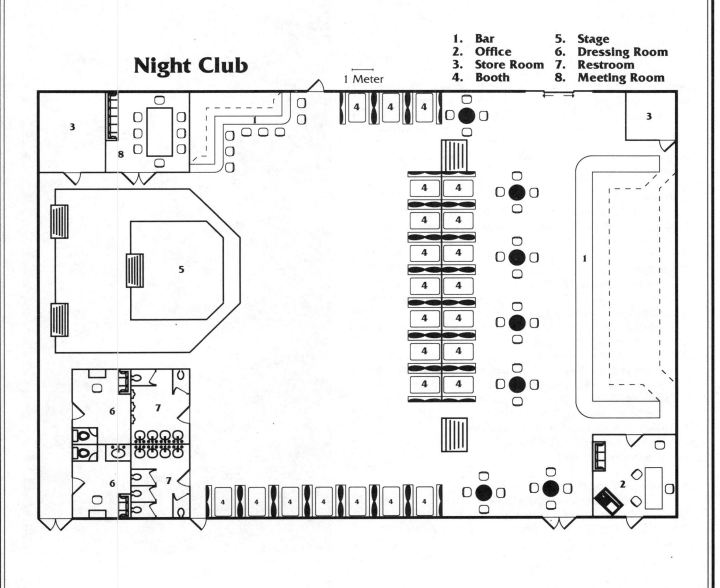

POLICE STATION

The typical police station is a two-story building, each floor being 50m x 50m. People entering the station on the first floor encounter a desk sergeant, who will direct them to the proper office. Down the corridor to the right are city government offices handling parking violations and other fines. To the left of the desk sergeant are the property officers who guard items recovered by the police until they are either returned to their owners or sent to the police evidence warehouse. Near the sergeant's desk are stairs and elevators leading up to the second floor. The rest of the first floor is used by patrol officers. Patrolmen can park their vehicles in a lot behind the station, then walk into a large reports room, where they do most of their "paper" work on one of many computer terminals. To either side of the reports room are smaller offices for the watch commander and his assistants. In one of these, the dispatcher monitors the station's computer and communications equipment.

A flight of stairs leads down from the report room to the basement, which contains six holding cells, each big and strong enough to hold up to two Troll suspects.

The second floor is for the precinct commander and detectives. The central area consists of a smaller reports room where detectives do most of their work. Encircling the offices of the precinct captain are various detective departments, archives with advanced computer facilities, interrogation rooms, and rooms where deckers stand watch over the precinct computer.

The elevators and stairs continue up to the roof, which is an all-weather helipad for police helicopters and tilt-rotor craft. A police air-traffic controller directs the police aircraft from a small control room on the roof.

Computer

Red-6, Trace and Report 4. At least one minor- or major-league decker is always standing guard over a police station computer.

Archetypes

Precinct Captain: Use **Detective**, p. 35, **SR**, with Biotech 3, Etiquette (Corporate) 5, Firearms 3, Interrogation 3, Leadership 3, Stealth 2, and Unarmed Combat 3.

Precinct Lieutenant: Use **Detective**, with Etiquette (Corporate) 4, Firearms 5, Interrogation 1, Leadership 1, Negotiation 4, Stealth 4, Unarmed Combat 4.

Precinct Detective: Use **Detective**, with Biotech 1, Car 4, Computer 3, Etiquette (Corporate) 2, Etiquette (Street) 3, Firearms 5, Negotiation 4, Stealth 4, Unarmed Combat 4.

Precinct Patrolman: Use **Street Cop**, p. 171, **SR**.

Clerical Staff: Use **Corporate Secretary**, p. 165, **SR**.

Typical Visitor: Anyone involved in a crime, whether as victim, witness, or suspect.

Number Of People Present

1 Captain, 2 Lieutenants, 1D6 +1 Detectives, 2D6 + 3 Patrolmen, 20 Clerical Staff, 1 Dispatcher, 2 Police Deckers, 1 Air Traffic Controller, 1D6 + 2 Suspects (4 in holding cells), 2D6 citizens.

Security

Police and security stations rely on equal measures of physical, electronic, and magical security. They can also call on a heavy security back-up in case of trouble. Magical backup tends to arrive fastest.

Police Station

1...Desk Sergeant
2...Main Entrance
3...Property Room
4...Stairs to Morgue and Cells

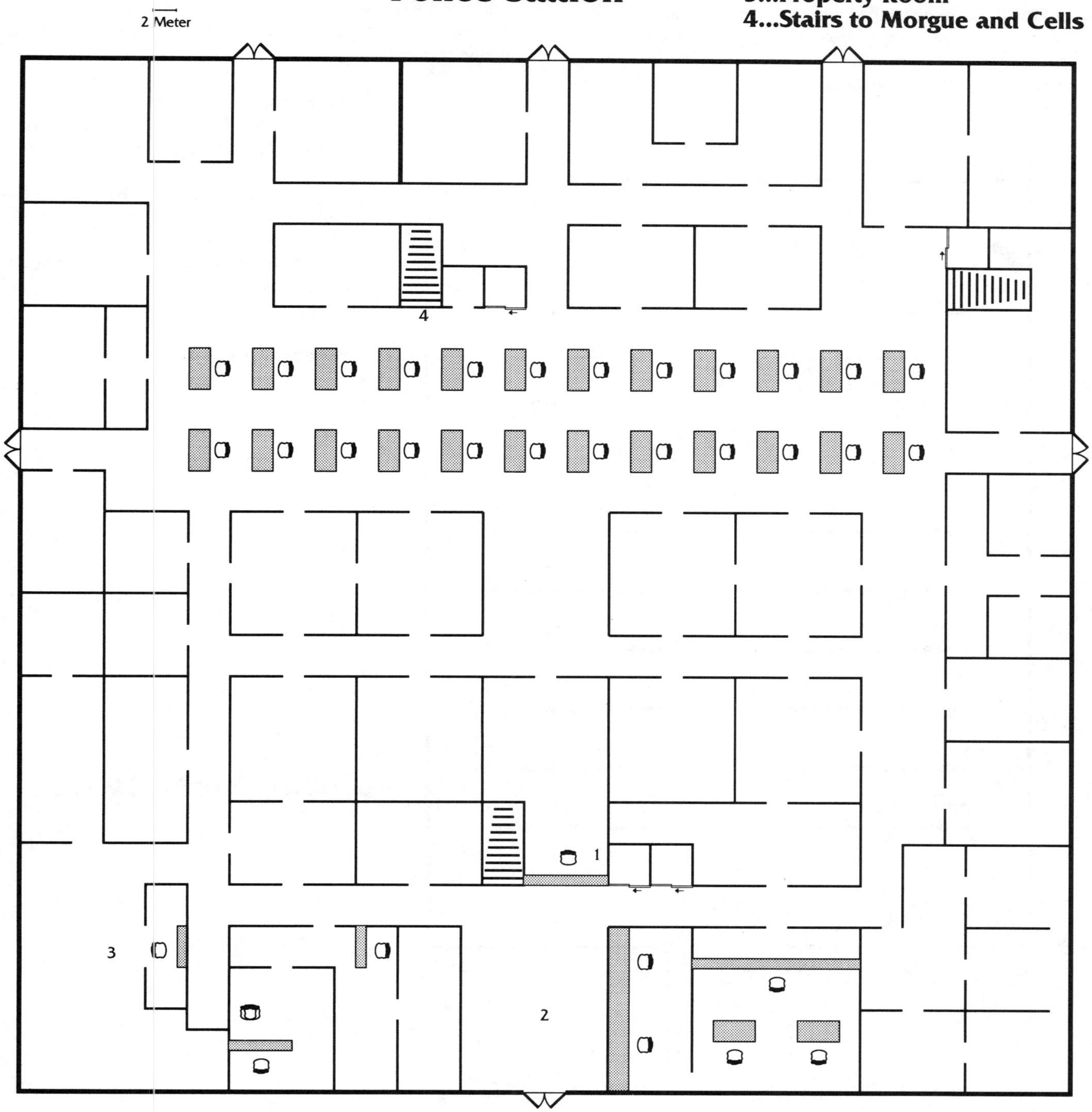

2 Meter

POLICLUB MEETING HALL

Because policlubs often represent unpopular views, some must meet in secret or in the poorest and most dangerous parts of the Sprawl. Policlub halls are usually abandoned school buildings or churches that the club may have either bought, rented, or seized. The polis usually renovate by plastering the exterior walls with their slogans and symbols. Inside, the walls are hung with huge posters of the policlub's leaders, more slogans, and religious and political symbols that represent the policlub's point of view.

The typical meeting hall is 15m x 10m, dirty, and two steps from total collapse (though exceptions also exist). Clubbers sit on old chairs, benches, and even pews, facing the podium as their leaders rant and rave about society's sins. Behind the po-

dium are small offices for the officers of the policlub. Near the entrances are stairs leading down to a basement where literature (and weapons, if the club is violently inclined) is stored.

Less radical, higher-profile policlubs use more public meeting places such as school auditoriums or public meeting halls. Use the same location map, but improve the general condition of the surroundings.

Computer

Orange-2 Access 3. Most policlubs take great pains to protect their computer systems. On the other hand, so many policlubs are suspicious of deckers and/or the poor, that a policlub computer's fearsome aspect might be only a mask to hide relatively minimal defenses.

Archetypes

Policlub Leader: Use **Gang Leader**, p. 167, **SR**, modifying listed skills according to type of policlub.

Policlub Officer: Use **Humanis Policlub Member**, p. 168, **SR**, with skills modified as above.

Policlub Members: Use **Humanis Policlub Member**, with skills modified as above.

Number Of People Present

1 Policlub Leader, 2 Policlub Officials, 3D6 Policlub Members.

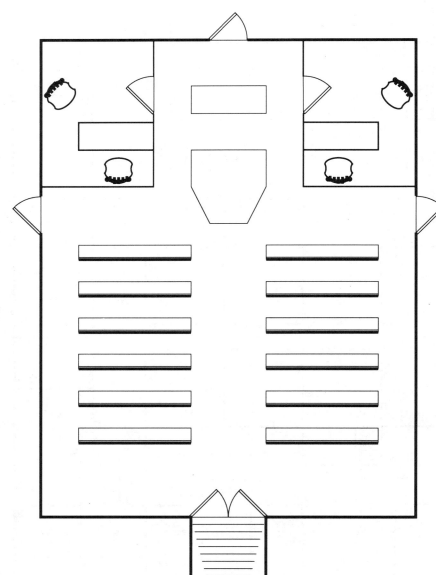

Policlub Meeting Hall

|—————|
1 Meter

RESIDENCE

Housing is at a premium in the Sprawl, because much of what exists is at the extremes between upper class mansions and century-old hovels.

Most apartment complexes have long waiting lists for the first available vacancy. In the effort to conserve space, most newer residential housing features sliding doors, built-in wall appliances, and so on. Half the apartment complexes are condominiums that usually require a down payment of one-fourth the selling price, with a 20-year mortgage on the rest.

Differences in lifestyle levels affect the personal services available to the apartment renter/owner. Those with a luxury lifestyle can count on free perks, such as security guards at their apartment door, free limousine service, cook and maid service, doubly secure computer lines, and free food. The building manager will scurry to provide just about anything for the luxury tenant. Those with a high-class lifestyle can obtain most services offered to the luxury types, but for a price. Those living in middle- and lower-class dwellings rarely find such services available.

SMALL RESIDENCE

A small residence consists of three rooms. The combination living room/kitchen (4m x 3m) has sofa, chairs, a small dining table, and kitchen appliances that slide in and out of the wall. The small half-bath (2.5m x 2m) has a toilet, sink, small dressing table, and a shower. The bedroom (3m x 2m) has just enough room for a queen-size bed, a few shelves, a closet, and a portable trideo. The more expensive small residences have a small patio (2m x.5m) extending from one side of the living room.

MEDIUM RESIDENCE

A medium apartment usually consists of five rooms. The entrance leads into a living room (6m x 5m) that usually leads out to a patio (3m x 5m). To the right of the living room is the kitchen (4m x 3m), which connects to a small dining area (3m x 3m). To the left of the living room is a small den or second bedroom (4m x 4m). To the left of the den are the bathroom (2m x 3m) and the master bedroom (4m x 4m).

Small Residence

1 Meter

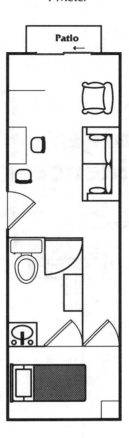

Medium Residence

1.5 Meters

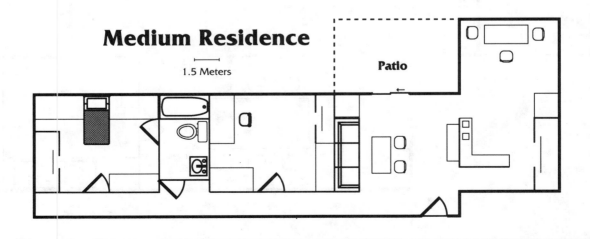

LARGE RESIDENCE

A large apartment also has five rooms. Entry is through a foyer (1.5m x 1.5m). The living room is large (10m x 7.5m) and often furnished fashionably and with an expensive entertainment system. The furnished patio (10m x 4m) has a wet bar. Off the living room are the dining room (5m x 4m) and the kitchen (5m x 4m). A hall leads from the dining room to the bathroom (4m x 3m), the den (4m x 3m), and the bedroom (6m x 5m).

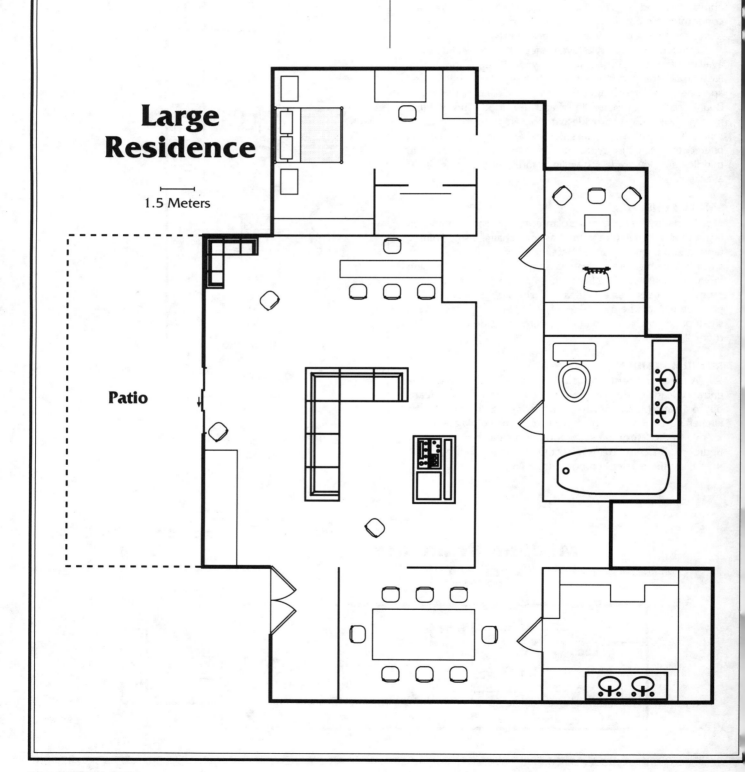

Large Residence

1.5 Meters

Patio

Security

Low Class: Strictly physical security devices, such as old-fashioned key locks, peep holes, and bars on windows.

Middle Class: Maglocks, tenant intercoms, strengthened doors, simple location violation alarm system.

High Class: Maglocks with thumbpad verification, video and intercom link with front door, identification scanner for guests, location violation alarm system linked to a central apartment security station. Guards.

Luxury Class: In addition to the high-class security measures, a luxury apartment owner knows that guards are at apartment complex gates, patrolling the outer walls, and at the doors to the building. The tenant can also ask for guards at his apartment door.

Hideout: Most crime syndicates and sophisticated criminals maintain hideouts. The hideout is usually a small-to-medium apartment or house in a poorer neighborhood. To ensure privacy and security, the owners install maglocks with retinal or thumbpad verification, video and intercom systems, bars on the windows, and specially coated wall paint or paper to prevent conversations being overheard in the next apartment.

Safe House: Governments and corporations use safe houses for protecting a valuable witness, as meeting places for agents, or as sites for conducting delicate or dangerous negotiations. A safe house is usually a large apartment or house in a wealthy neighborhood, where privacy is valued. Sophisticated security devices watch over every room and every possible approach to the safe house. The devices are usually monitored away from the house. Guards patrol the approaches to the house and are posted at the door and outside the windows.

Computer

Low Class: Does not have a centralized computer network. Computer security is strictly the tenant's responsibility.

Middle Class: **Green-2 Access 3.** A simple centralized computer network.

High Class: **Green-5 Barrier 4.** A more sophisticated computer network.

Luxury Class: **Orange-3, Barrier 5, Trace and Burn 3.** Also has a major-league decker riding the system.

Archetypes

Low-Class Apartment Manager: Use **Corporate Official**, p. 107, this book, with Etiquette (Corporate) 2, Etiquette (Street) 2, Negotiation 2, Computer 1.

Middle-Class Apartment Manager: Use **Corporate Official**, with Etiquette (Corporate) 3, Etiquette (Street) 1, Negotiation 2, Computer 2.

High-Class Apartment Manager: Use **Corporate Official**, with Etiquette (Corporate) 3, Etiquette (Media) 2, Negotiation 3, Computer 2.

Luxury-Class Apartment Manager: Use **Corporate Official**, with Etiquette (Corporate) 3, Etiquette (Media) 3, Negotiation 3, Computer 3.

RESIDENCE COSTS TABLE

Small Apartment (Furnished)

	To Rent/Month	To Own
Low Class	250¥	20,000¥
Middle Class	450¥	38,000¥
High Class	1000¥	82,000¥
Luxury Class	(Usually Not Available)	

Medium Apartment (Furnished)

	To Rent/Month	To Own
Low Class	350¥	40,000¥
Middle Class	600¥	70,000¥
High Class	1200¥	140,000¥
Luxury Class	2000¥	230,000¥

Large Apartment (Furnished)

	To Rent/Month	To Own
Low Class	(Usually not available)	
Middle Class	900¥/	105,000¥
High Class	1900¥	220,000¥
Luxury Class	3800¥	500,000¥

Number Of People Present

The following assumes a single 20-story apartment building.

Low Class: 1 Manager, 1 Assistant Manager, 1 Mechanic, 3 Entrance Guards, 600 tenants (20 apartments/floor x 20 floors x 1.5 people).

Middle Class: 1 Manager, 2 Assistant Managers, 2 Mechanics, 6 Entrance Guards, 20 Floor Guards, 450 Tenants (15 apartments/floor x 20 floors x 1.5 people).

High Class: 1 Manager, 4 Assistant Managers, 4 Mechanics, 10 Maids and Cooks, 4 Patrolling Guards, 6 Entrance Guards, 20 Floor Guards, 300 Tenants (10 apartments/floor x 20 floors x 1.5 people).

Luxury Class: 1 Manager, 4 Assistant Managers, 4 Mechanics, 20 Maids and Cooks, 12 Patrolling Guards, 12 Entrance Guards, 40 Floor Guards, 240 Tenants (8 apartments/floor x 20 floors x 1.5 people

RESTAURANT

FAST FOOD/SMALL RESTAURANT

Such restaurants are usually 10m x 20m, with the food preparation area taking up almost half the available space. Behind the counters of fast-food restaurants and behind the kitchen doors of small restaurants are microwave ovens, UV cookers, conventional ovens, and large refrigerators for heating and serving pre-packaged foods. The restaurant's owner has his or her offices to the rear of the kitchen, usually near the door leading to the back alley or parking lot.

The decor of fast-food restaurants is usually plastic and wood veneer, while the decor of privately owned, small restaurants is more imaginative. Small restaurants have up to twelve tables.

Computer

Green-4, Barrier 2. Limited to storing information on current sales, inventory, and personnel records.

Archetypes

Owner: Use **Bartender**, p. 163, **SR**, with Etiquette (Corporate) 1, Etiquette (Street) 2 (Fast Food Manager only), and Special Skill of Street Rumormill 1.

Wait Staff: Use **Corporate Secretary**, p. 165, **SR**, with Etiquette (Street) 1 and Street Rumormill 2.

Cooks: Use **Corporate Secretary**, with Etiquette (Street) 1, Street Rumormill 1, and Food Preparation 1.

Restaurant Guard: Use **Corporate Security Guard**, p. 165, **SR**.

Typical Patron: Anyone with money and no obvious diseases.

Number Of People Present

1 Owner/Manager, 6 Waiters, 1 Cook, 1 Guard, 2 D6 – 2 Customers.

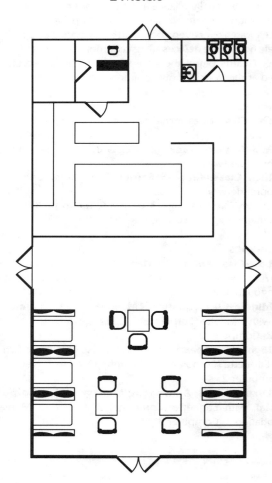

Small Restaurant

2 Meters

MID-SIZE RESTAURANT

A mid-size restaurant takes up an area 15m x 30m. The kitchen area is 10m x 15m and is capable of preparing more complex foods than the smaller, fast food restaurants. A mid-size eatery can afford to create an atmosphere suited to the menu offered. Mid-size restaurants can have up to 20 tables and sometimes a small bar.

Computer

Green-6, Access 5. Limited to storing information on current sales, inventory, and personnel records.

Archetypes

Owner: Use **Bartender**, p. 163, **SR**, with Etiquette (Corporate) 2, Etiquette (Street) 2, and Street Rumormill 1.

Wait Staff: Use **Corporate Secretary**, p. 165, **SR**, with Etiquette (Street) 3, Unarmed Combat 1, Street Rumormill 2.

Cooks: Use **Corporate Secretary**, with Etiquette (Street) 1, Street Rumormill 1, Food Preparation 2.

Restaurant Guard: Use **Corporate Security Guard**, p. 165, **SR**.

Typical Customer: Any class person who meets minimum dress standards.

Number Of People Present

1 Owner/Manager, 2 Cooks, 8 Waiters, 2 Guards, 2D6 + 1 Customers.

Medium Restaurant

2 Meters

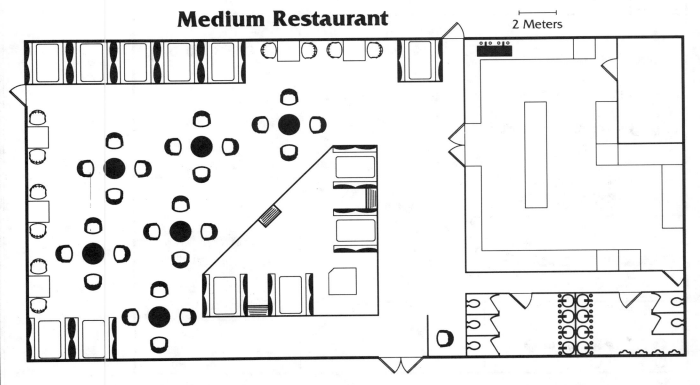

LARGE RESTAURANT

Large restaurants are 30m x 30m and larger. Most cater to the upper classes, though some serve other classes. The food preparation area has everything needed to prepare complex meals for many people. A large restaurant often has a bar. Owners usually spare no expense in decorating the restaurant's interior or in putting together a staff of courteous and discreet employees. A large restaurant holds up to 40 tables divided among several rooms.

Computer

Orange-3, Access 6. Computer information is limited to current sales, inventory, and personnel records.

Archetypes

Owner: Use **Bartender**, p. 163, **SR**, with Etiquette (Corporate) 3, Etiquette (Street) 1, Etiquette (Media) 2, and Special Skills of Corporate Rumormill 4 and Media Rumormill 1.

Wait Staff: Use **Corporate Secretary**, p. 165, **SR**, with Charisma 5, Etiquette (Corporate) 2, Etiquette (Media) 1, Etiquette (Street) 1, Unarmed Combat (to dodge feely customers) 1, and Special Skills of Media Rumormill 1, Corporate Rumormill 2.

Cooks: Use **Corporate Secretary**, with Etiquette (Corporate) 1 and Special Skills of Corporate Rumormill 2 and Food Preparation 3.

Restaurant Guard: Use **Corporate Security Guard**, p. 165, **SR**.

Typical Patron: Usually individuals from the middle and upper classes.

Number Of People Present

1 Owner/Manager, 3 Cooks, 12 Waiters, 3 Guards, 4D6 Customers.

Large Restaurant

2 Meters

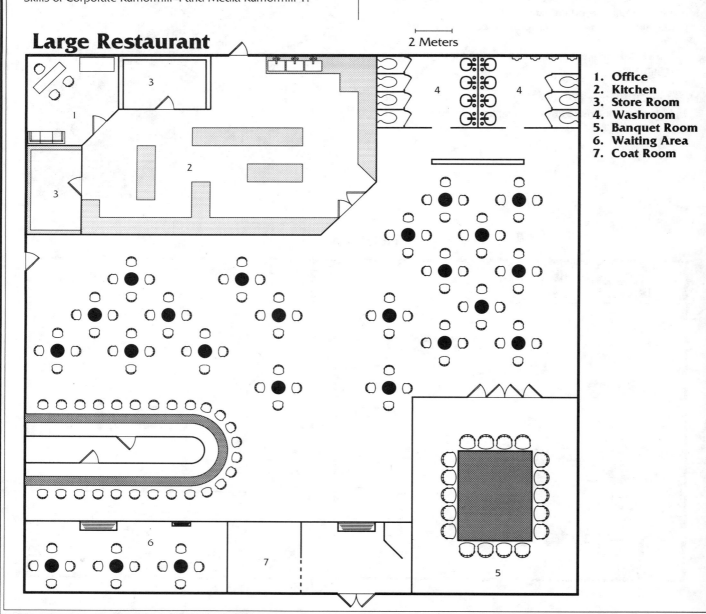

1. **Office**
2. **Kitchen**
3. **Store Room**
4. **Washroom**
5. **Banquet Room**
6. **Waiting Area**
7. **Coat Room**

SHOPPING MALL

A shopping mall is a collection of various-size stores built under a common roof. Most malls usually have two large stores and two medium-size stores separated by 15 to 30 small specialty stores (See **Stores**, p. 40ff, for dimensions). Malls also have at least two small restaurants (usually fast-food) and at least one small bank. The only stores to which most mall management organizations will not lease space are weapons stores or those catering overtly to sexual fantasies. All malls have good access to a city's public transportation, as well as parking for private vehicles. A helipad for public and private helicopters and tilt-rotor craft serves the affluent.

The private offices of the mall association are usually placed above the crowds in the plaza. A system of corridors connects the offices and the rear of the stores with each other and the mall's loading docks. These corridors are open only to store staff and mall security personnel.

The mall has a large stake in tight security. So many people present in such a confined space has more than once served the gruesome purposes of both psychotics and political terrorists. Thus do malls employ many guards and install major security systems.

Computer

Orange-6, Trace and Burn 4. The mall association computer runs the security system and environmental systems, and receives information from the store computers via their "backdoor" system access nodes.

Archetypes

Mall Association President: Use **Corporate Official**, p. 107, this book, with Leadership 2.

Other Officials and Secretaries: Use **Corporate Official** and **Corporate Secretary**, p. 165, **SR**.

Security Chief: Use **Corporate Security Guard**, p. 165, **SR**, with Etiquette (Corporate) 3, Etiquette (Street) 1, Firearms 4, Interrogation 3, Leadership 2, and Unarmed Combat 4.

Watch Commander: Use **Corporate Security Guard**, with Etiquette (Corporate) 2, Etiquette (Street) 1, Firearms 4, Interrogation 2, Leadership 1, and Unarmed Combat 4.

Mall Guards: Use **Corporate Security Guard**.

Typical Customer: Anyone with nuyen and a shirt and shoes.

Number Of People Present

1 Mall President, 2 Mall Officials, 5 Secretaries, 1 Security Chief, 1 Watch Commander, 30 Mall Guards (15 in uniforms, 15 in plain clothes), 163 Store Personnel, 1D6 x 100 Customers.

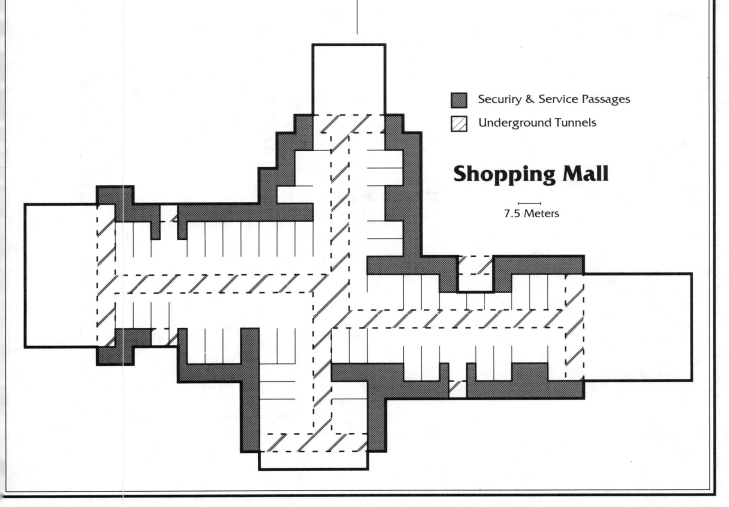

■ Securiry & Service Passages

▨ Underground Tunnels

Shopping Mall

⊢——⊣
7.5 Meters

STORE

The first three locations are for generic small, medium, and large stores. Three specific store archetypes (Tech Store, Talisman Store, and Simsense Store) follow immediately after.

SMALL STORE

A typical small store is 7m x 25m. The credchecker is next to the entrance. Long shelves line one wall, while smaller shelves and bins line the other. Midway in is a short stairway that leads up to the second floor or down to a small storage area. The best items for sale are displayed in a long glass case at the rear of the store. An exit into the back alley is in a rear corner.

Computer

Small stores usually rely on desktop or similar small systems for their computing needs. Only rarely does one require a system that accesses the local Grid.

Archetypes

Manager: Use **Corporate Official**, p. 107, this book, with Computer 1, Etiquette (Corporate) 1, Etiquette (Street) 1, Negotiation 2.

Sales Staff: Use **Corporate Wage Slave**, p. 108, this book.

Store Guard: Use **Corporate Security Guard**, p. 165, **SR**.

Number Of People Present

1 Manager, 3 Salespersons, 1 Guard, 1D6 – 1 Customers.

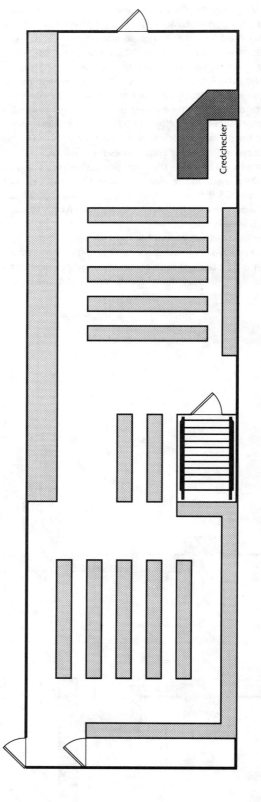

Credchecker

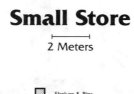

Small Store

|————|
2 Meters

▨ Shelves & Bins

MEDIUM STORE

A medium store averages 35m x 60m in size. There are usually two customer entrances, with wide aisles dividing the interior into quarters. Each quarter displays a general group of products (electronics, foods, and so on). The more expensive items are in display cases along the walls. Two or more sets of stairs usually lead to a basement and to upstairs offices, where the security chief monitors electronic surveillance. Credcheckers are located near the doors. There are also several storerooms, one of which leads to the loading bay, where trucks disgorge the day's merchandise.

Computer

Orange-3, Trace and Dump 3. Little more than local Grid access nodes, a medium store's computer system contains rudimentary network systems linking all credstick checker and inventory control systems. Information necessary for credit checks and so on is done by communication with the credit agency.

Archetypes

Manager: Use **Corporate Official**, p. 107, this book, with Computer 2, Etiquette (Corporate) 2, Etiquette (Street) 1, and Negotiation 3.

Assistant Manager: Use **Corporate Official**, with Computer 2, Etiquette (Corporate) 1, Etiquette (Street) 1, and Negotiation 2.

Sales Staff: Use **Corporate Wage Slave**, p. 108, this book.

Store Guard: Use **Corporate Security Guard**, p. 165, this book.

Number Of People Present

1 Manager, 1 Assistant Manager, 8 Salespeople, 2 Guards, 3D6 – 3 Customers.

Medium Store

■ Shelves & Bins

4 Meters

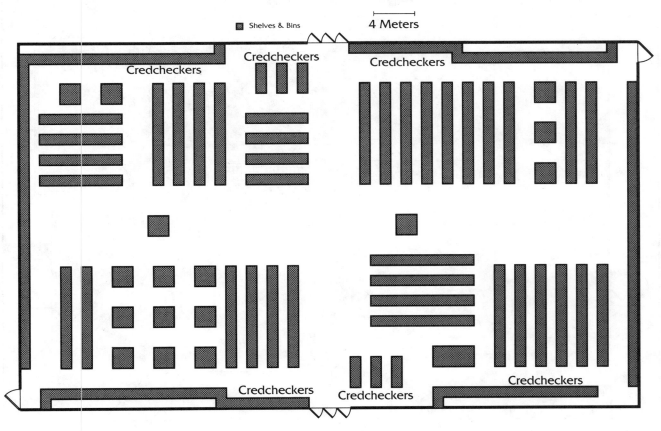

Credcheckers

Credcheckers

Credcheckers

Credcheckers

Credcheckers

Credcheckers

LARGE STORE

A large store is at least 60m x 80m in size, and many have more than one floor. There are usually two wide entrances. The store is divided into areas, each selling particular items such as women's clothing, trideo sets, and so on. Each area has its own credchecker. In multi-floor stores, escalators are located centrally and elevators near the store's entrances. Large department stores usually have large, well-protected parking garages, either on the roof or underground. Some luxury department stores have helipads to allow the helicopters of rich clientele to avoid the city streets.

Computer

Orange-5, Trace and Burn 4. A large store's computer system is a complicated network interlinking the retail and administrative departments of the store. If the store is not part of a chain, credit and personnel records are stored in-house. If part of a chain, valuable information such as credit histories is stored at the main headquarters.

Archetypes

Manager: Use **Corporate Official**, p. 107, this book, with Computer 3, Etiquette (Corporate) 3, Etiquette (Street) 1, and Negotiation 4.

Assistant Manager: Use **Corporate Official**, with Computer 2, Etiquette (Corporate) 2, Etiquette (Street) 1, and Negotiation 3.

Security Chief: Use **Corporate Security Guard**, p. 165, **SR**, with Computer 2 and Electronics 2.

Sales Staff: Use **Corporate Wage Slave**, p. 108, this book.

Store Guard: Use **Corporate Security Guard**.

Number Of People Present

1 Manager, 2 Assistant Managers, 18 Salespeople, 1 Security Chief, 10 Guards (4 in uniform, 10 in plain clothes), 1D6 x 7 Customers.

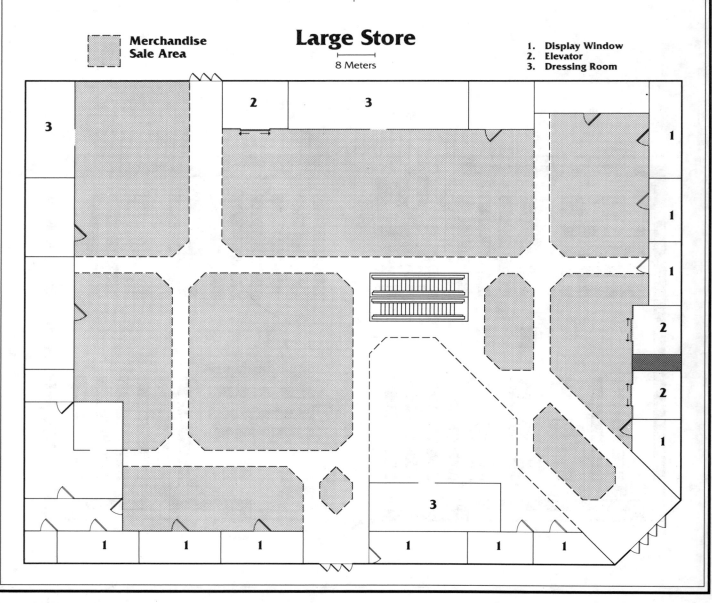

Merchandise Sale Area

Large Store

8 Meters

1. Display Window
2. Elevator
3. Dressing Room

SHADOW TECH STORE

The shadow tech store sells and services computers and other high-technology equipment, and also specializes in under-the-counter illegal items. If the store's owner deals in illegal software or hardware, he will sell it to a runner he knows and trusts. For physical dimensions, see either **Small** or **Medium Store**.

For all intents and purposes, the shadow tech store resembles a general high-tech store.

Computer

Red-7, Barrier 5, Blaster 5. Because shadow tech stores sell hard and software to people who may use it to commit computer crimes, the government deckers make frequent incursions into their datastores. As protection, the store owners have commissioned some of the fiercest computer defenses around. Owners and their technicians are usually major-league deckers (or at least experienced minor-league deckers).

Archetypes

Owner: Use **Decker**, p. 34, **SR**, with Computer 4, Computer (B/R) 4, Computer Theory 4, Electronics 4, Etiquette (Corporate) 1, and Etiquette (Street) 4.

Salesman: Use **Decker**, with Computer 3, Computer (B/R) 2, Computer Theory 3, Electronics 2, Etiquette (Corporate) 1, and Etiquette (Street) 3.

Technician: Use **Technician**, p. 120, this book.

Typical Customer: Any decker or would-be decker is on a first-name basis with the owner and salespeople of the local shadow tech store. Anyone with an interest in advanced electronics is also a potential client.

Number Of People Present

1 Owner, 2 Salesmen, 1 Technician, 2 Guards, 1D6 – 2 Customers.

SIMSENSE STORE

Though most simsense stores are small, they can carry hundreds of simsense recordings (the size of a human palm), headsets, and accessories. Recordings are grouped by type (romantic, historical, sports, and so on) and simstars (Caroline New York, Metal Merlin, et al). Adult subject recordings are kept in the rear of the store behind the display case with the simsense headsets. Most simsense stores also carry a rack of fan datafiles and magazines. When a new recording comes out, store owners must hire extra guards to prevent the crowds from wrecking the store in their frenzy to obtain copies of a new simsense release featuring a popular star.

Computer

Green-5, Access 6. A simsense store computer contains routine inventory listings and personnel records. The only information of importance would be the expected release dates of the next hot simsense recording.

Archetypes

Store Owner: Use **Corporate Official**, p.107, this book, with Etiquette (Corporate) 1, Etiquette (Media) 3, Etiquette (Street) 1, Knowledge of Simsense Scene 5, Negotiation 2.

Sale Staff: Use **Fan**, p. 110, this book. Add Special Skill of Media Rumormill 1.

Typical Customer: Use **Fan**.

Number Of People Present

1 Store Owner, 1 Salesperson, 1 Guard (3 when major recording comes out), 2D6 Customers, or 2D6 x 10 for a new release.

TALISMAN SHOP

A talisman shop, or lore store, sells magical goods. The shelves display mostly trinkets whose minor spells provide more a psychological boost for their owners rather than anything really magical. The genuine and powerful items are kept well out of sight and away from sticky fingers.

The average lore store is small (see p. 40), with its wares in display cases and shelves. Such a shop also carries books about magic, though none of any worth to shamans and mages. Again, the truly valuable items are kept either locked away in a secret vault in a storeroom or in a special display case at the rear of the store. If the owner knows and trusts a client, he will offer these special items, provide information, or put the customer in touch with other magicians.

Computer

Orange-3, Barrier 4. Most magicians, even talismongers, tend to shy away from anything electronic, but the talisman shop owner must use a computer to keep track of the multiple aspects of his store. It is equally important to keep this information safe.

Archetypes

Shop Owner: Use **Talismonger**, p. 172, **SR**, with Etiquette (Corporate) 1, Etiquette (Tribal) 2, and Special Skills of Metalworking 2 and Woodworking 2.

Salesman: Use **Talismonger** with Etiquette (Corporate) 1, Enchantment 3, Etiquette (Street) 3, Etiquette (Tribal) 1, Magical Theory 6, Negotiation 4, Sorcery 3, and Special Skills of Metalworking 2 and Woodworking 2.

Guard: Use **Corporate Security Guard**, p. 165, **SR**, with Etiquette (Corporate) 1, Etiquette (Street) 3, Firearms 3, Unarmed Combat 3.

Typical Customer: Regulars tend to be Mages, p. 45, **SR**, and occasionally Shamans, p. 44, **SR**.

Number Of People Present

1 Owner, 1 Assistant, 1 Guard, 1D6 −1 Customers.

WEAPON STORE

A weapon store is a medium store (p. 41) that sells all manner of weaponry. Weapons and ammunition are kept in locked display cases or in locked racks on the wall. Accessories such as scopes, tools, and clothing are also available, but are more accessible to customers. A larger store may have a shooting range so that customers can try out weapons.

Illegal firearms (machine guns, missile systems, and such) are usually only for sale when the owner knows the customer well enough or if the customer is willing to pay a high enough price. The store will have some illegal weapons in hidden racks, but special requests must be ordered through any connections the store owner has.

Security for a weapon store is *extremely* tight. In addition to guards, every salesperson carries a sidearm and has access to heavier weaponry behind the counters. Customers must be buzzed in through a set of armor glass double doors, and very often a guard frisks them at the door before they can enter any further.

Computer

Orange-4, Trace and Dump 4. Beyond inventory and employee records, a weapon store's computer contains a list of weapons sources. Those sources are not always particularly legit.

Archetypes

Store Owner: Use **Ork Mercenary**, p. 41, **SR**. Subtract 1 from Body, Strength, and all skills. Add 1 to Intelligence.

Salestaff: Use **Corporate Wage Slave**, p. 108, this book. Add Firearms 2.

Guards: Use **Corporate Security Guard**, p. 165, **SR**.

Typical Customer: Anyone wanting to protect himself or who is fascinated by weapons.

Number Of People Present

1 Store Owner, 10 Salestaff, 4 Guards, 2D6 –1 Customers.

SPRAWL ENCOUNTERS

The gamemaster can use the descriptions in this section as a guideline for creating the many types of encounters and incidents that can occur in neighborhoods of the Sprawl. Each encounter falls into a type such as Gang, Magic, Underworld, and so on, but the individual incidents are general enough that gamemasters can tailor them to their own campaigns or player groups.

GENERATING ENCOUNTERS

Each encounter takes place in a particular neighborhood, and each neighborhood is assigned a Security Rating, with AAA being at the top of the scale and Z being the most god-forsaken area of the Sprawl. The Enforcement Table on p. 124 of this book explains the eight categories in more detail.

Having decided on the Security Rating of the neighborhood where the encounter will take place, the gamemaster rolls 2D6 against the Master Encounter Table. Let's say he rolls a 5 against Security Rating B, resulting in a Gang Encounter Type. Now he goes to the Incident Table and rolls 1D6 against Gang Encounters. He gets a 6, narrowing it further to a Go-Gang Encounter. To determine which of the six Go-Gang incidents will happen, he rolls 1D6 one more time.

MASTER ENCOUNTER TABLE (ROLL 2D6)

AAA Rating Die Roll	Encounter Type	C Rating	
2 – 3	Police/Security Encounter	2	Upper Class Encounter
4 – 6	Upper Class Encounter	3	Racial Encounter
7 – 9	Racial Encounter	4 – 6	Police/Security Encounter
10	Magic Encounter	7 – 8	Gang Encounter
11	Other Encounter	9	Underworld Encounter
12	Gang Encounter	10 – 11	Magic Encounter
		12	Other Encounter
AA Rating		**D Rating**	
2	Upper Class Encounter	2	Upper Class Encounter
3 – 5	Police/Security Encounter	3	Racial Encounter
6 – 7	Racial Encounter	4 – 6	Police/Security Encounter
8 – 9	Underworld Encounter	7 – 9	Gang Encounter
10	Magic Encounter	10	Underworld Encounter
11	Other Encounter	11	Magic Encounter
12	Gang Encounter	12	Other Encounter
A Rating		**E Rating**	
2	Upper Class Encounter	2	Upper Class Encounter
3 – 5	Gang Encounter	3	Racial Encounter
6 – 7	Police/Security Encounter	4 – 5	Police/Security Encounter
8 – 9	Underworld Encounter	6 – 8	Gang Encounter
10	Racial Encounter	9 – 10	Underworld Encounter
11	Magic Encounter	11	Magic Encounter
12	Other Encounter	12	Other Encounter
B Rating		**Z Rating**	
2	Upper Class Encounter	2	Racial Encounter
3 – 5	Gang Encounter	3 – 5	Police/Security Encounter
6 – 7	Police/Security Encounter	6 – 9	Gang Encounter
8 – 9	Underworld Encounter	10 – 11	Underworld Encounter
10	Racial Encounter	12	Magic Encounter
11	Magic Encounter		
12	Other Encounter		

INCIDENT TABLE (ROLL 1D6)

Gang Encounters

1 – 2	Gang 1, pp.50-51
3 – 4	Gang 2, pp. 52-53
5	Gang 3, pp. 54-55
6	Go-Gang, pp. 56-57

Police/Security Encounters

1-3	Sprawl Police 1, pp. 76-77
4 – 5	Corp Police 1, pp. 72-73
6	Corp Police 2, pp. 74-75

Upper Class Encounters

1 – 2	Celebrity, pp. 66-67
3 – 4	Media, pp. 68-69
5 – 6	Corp Folk, pp. 70-71

Racial Encounters

1	Dwarf, pp. 82-83
2 – 3	Elf, pp. 84-85
4 – 5	Ork, pp. 88-89
6	Troll, pp. 86-87

Underworld Encounters

1 – 3	Mafia, pp. 60-61
4 – 6	Yakuza, pp.62-63

Magic Encounters

1 – 3	Magic 1, pp. 78-79
4 – 6	Magic 2, pp. 80-81

Other Encounters

1	Rich Folks, pp. 64-65
2 – 3	Night Spot, pp. 58-59
4 – 5	Policlub, pp. 90-91
6	Technology, pp.92-93

A kid with spiked hair and a gang tattoo on his cheek. Dressed shabbily but carries no visible weapon.

Quotes

"Hey, chummer, looking for some action?"

"You with some group or you just hanging out? Hey, just asking!"

"I'm thinking of starting an association of my own. Birds of a feather, right? Interested?"

Notes:

After being passed over in a recent spate of gang promotions, this kid wants to put together his own gang. He may not have thought it through fully, but he's got some smarts.

If the group refuses him in the right manner, he'll follow and be there to help the characters out of trouble. If they act aggressively toward him, he'll go to his gang to make trouble for the party. He'll probably suggest that the gang shadow the party, then hit them after they finish their run.

He's got rudimentary combat skills, with a knife his weapon of choice. He also knows some decking.

Archetypes

Kid: Use **Gang Boss**, p.167, **SR** rules. Reduce all skills by half and subtract 1 from each attribute except Essence. Unarmed Combat becomes 3.

Gang Members: Use **Gang Boss** as above, but arm these characters with light pistols or hand weapons.

Info/Contacts

This kid knows everything about the neighborhood and a good deal about the local corps, especially information related to pilfering or stealing.

A young girl, blond and scarecrow-thin. She is pretty, except for a black eye and a split lip.

Quotes

"Wanna see a good time, chummer? I'll be your friend if you want. Honest. I'll be good for you."

"I am not a runaway! My parents know exactly where I am...Sort of."

"Please, you gotta. If you don't help me, I'll be in big trouble. You'll like it, I promise."

Notes

This girl is a runaway who recently made it to the Sprawl on a Blueline Bus. She's been through some rough treatment from the local gang. They abused her, and now they've sent her out to earn her keep on the street.

The gang has threatened to contact her folks if she refuses to work for them. This scares her more than the gang, because her father is a powerful corporator who terrorized his wife and children for years. When Mom had an accident and died—soon to be replaced by a younger woman—the girl decided to run.

She is in such dire straits that suicide is a possibility. The runners may decide to nursemaid her, even though it would offer them little in return. Her information on the gang and her father's corp might somehow prove of value, but she offers not much else.

Archetypes

Girl: Use **Corporate Wage Slave**, p. 107, this book. Raise Charisma to 3 and Willpower to 2.

Father: Use **Mr. Johnson**, p. 170, **SR** rules.

Gang Members: Use **Squatter**, p. 170, **SR** rules.

Info/Contacts

The only people the girl knows in the Sprawl are the gang members. As far as her father's corp, she knows some access codes and has heard about a bioengineering program.

A tall, unwashed young gang soldier. His face is acne-scarred and his front tooth chipped. Very tough.

Quotes

"Hey, chummer, you look ready for trouble. If the price is right, we might want to buy a sample."

"Gonna get wet around here, and we ain't talking rain, chummer. You wanna be a cutter or a leaker?"

"Ever make idiot wine? Find a gang moving in on your turf and stomp 'em."

Notes

Because of predation by Lone Star and by other local gangs, the gang on this turf is slightly undermanned. A rival gang is trying to drive them from their territory, placing them under serious pressure.

This ganger wants to hire some extra help for the short term. He's not really thought about getting out of the gang, which is good, because he'd never be a decent runner. If the characters help him now, he will return the favor later.

Archetypes

Mid-Level Soldier: Use **Gang Member**, p. 39, **SR**.

Other Gang Members: Use **Gang Member**. The soldier's gang numbers about 13. The rivals have roughly double that. With help, the underdogs should win any rumble, with minimum losses.

Info/Contacts

The Gang Soldier is a pro at street-level crimes such as mugging, theft, and loan sharking. If the players' team does not help him, he will nail them just when they don't need more trouble.

Lean and unkempt, the Gang Boss has haunted, bloodshot eyes that tell you he's addicted to something.

Quotes

"You ain't squat if you ain't one of us, chummer. You don't breathe here without my say-so. Got it?"

"Magic? That's crapola the corps spread around to keep us in our place. Magic is a gun, and I'm a mage."

"If you can see it, you can shoot it. If you can shoot it, you can kill it. If it dies, it ain't tough."

Notes

This guy's problem is not just the BTL chips he's jacking every hour. He is an untrained Shaman who recently met his totem animal, an enormous, hairy spider sitting in the middle of a web. It scared hell out of him.

He's been fighting to deny the vision, which is how he became a chiphead. Half out of his brain, he has been ordering gang members to step up their activities so he can pay for his addiction. His underlings are planning to rebel, which he has learned from visions sent by his spider totem.

Archetypes

Gang Boss: Use **Gang Boss**, p. 167, **SR**. Give him a Magic Pool of 1 automatically used for his own defense.

Gang Members: Use **Gang Member**, p. 39, **SR** rules, for up to two dozen of the motley crew.

Info/Contacts

Like his totem spider, this man is at the center of a web of low-level contacts within the neighborhood and organized crime.

If the players don't help him, he becomes enraged. The Gang Boss's meltdown could easily involve everyone in its random violence.

The Gang Enforcer is a whipcord-lean woman. Cold smile, colder eyes, and voice with a razor edge.

Quotes

"Whatchu doing here, chummer? Wrong answer. The right answer is, 'I'm leaving right now.'"

"My time's too valuable to kill you. You ain't worth the sawdust it would take to sop up your juices."

"Yeah, I got a bullet with your name on it. All mine have 'Spaz' stamped on them. Getoutahere."

Notes

This gang enforcer is charged with assaying threats to the gang and "inviting" them to leave the area. She thinks the players' team looks like a capable crew, which is why she's trying to bluff them into leaving. Her normal operating proce-dure would be to haul intruders out back and beat the hell out of them.

If the players' team can convince her of their neutrality, she'll let them stay as long as there is no trouble. If there is trouble, she'll offer them a chance to leave or to join up with her gang to meet the threat.

If she takes a shine to the group because of their snappy repartee, she'll cut them some slack, and would even run interference if things got tight on a run. She'd never admit that up front, however.

Archetypes

Gang Enforcer: Use **Street Samurai**, p. 46, **SR** rules.

Gang Members: Use **Gang Member**, p. 39, **SR** rules, for up to 24.

Info/Contacts

Because of her suspicious nature, the Gang Enforcer is somewhat isolated. She knows some fixers and has done a run or two far from her own turf, so she might have info that could help the player characters with a job of their own.

The Gang Boss is tall and charismatically handsome, though his look is plenty tough. Restless eyes and a plastic smile.

Quotes

"I think we can reach an understanding, chummer. More nuyen, the more I understand."

"Hey, I'm only warning you about the corp hit team 'cause I don't want you splashed on my turf."

"We'll provide back-up and smoke for a 40 percent cut. It's fair, and you can afford it."

Notes

This Gang Boss is the ultimate manipulator. He constantly stirs up trouble between his subordinates to prevent them from developing a coalition to challenge his power. He also foments conflicts between enemy gangs to keep them weak with continual battling.

The key to his success is that all his lies contain a kernel of truth. He wants to control the players' group, for he feels threatened by any power he senses in others. If he can persuade the team to go after another gang or some corp cops, he wins twice.

Archetypes

Gang Boss: Use **Gang Boss**, p. 167, **SR** rules. He carries an Ares Predator.

Gang Members (12): Use **Gang Member**, p. 39, **SR**.

Info/Contacts

The Gang Boss has a feel for the political undercurrents in the city, but it is impossible to get information out of him unless what the players want to know will set them against one of his foes.

He can afford to wait. If he can't direct the team against someone, he can send someone against them. They are, after all, on his turf. Here, he's king. Forget that at your peril.

As the runners are quietly going about their business, a group of street punks decides to have a little fun. Boy, are they in for a surprise!

Quotes

"Hoi, high 'n mighty. Recognize this?" (shotgun)

"The kind o' trouble you can gimme? I ain't scared o' your mommy, chummer."

"What's a looker like you doing with a mug like him? C'mon, let's play joytoy."

Notes

The Royal Reapers are out on Ronin turf, making sure that everyone knows that the Reapers are the new force in the plex. The Ronins are on Shamrock turf tonight, else the Reapers'd be singing soprano by now.

Archetypes

Six Reapers: four Princes and two Princesses.

Roscoe, late teens, a thorough punk. Use **Gang Member**, p. 39, **SR** rules, with Fichetti 500 (10 shot clip).

Roamer, age 12 or 13, tries to act tough. Use **Bartender**, p. 163, **SR** rules, without Special Skills.

Rocker is in his mid-teens, with silvered hair and real leather clothes. Usually dead to the world, listening to his 'toid amps. Use **Rocker**, p. 43, **SR** rules, with a Streetline Special.

Glitter wants to be a Rocker and dresses the part. Every piece of clothing is light blue, as is his hair. A glitter-painted star glints from his left cheek. Use **Rocker** p. 43, **SR**, with a Remington Roomsweeper.

Shirley hangs on Roscoe, and tries to act like him. Use **Gang Member**, p. 39, **SR**.

Shiv is the deadliest of all, a borderline psychotic who is silent except when attacking with a banshee yell. Use **Gang Boss**, p. 167, **SR**, with Retractable Spurs.

Info/Contacts

There are other teams of Reapers fanning out. If the runners are looking for anything in Reaper or Ronin turf, the Reapers can help them find it tonight. Any of the Reapers is a valuable contact into the gang.

The runners are moving down the street, trying to trail a suit, when they notice some punks in green smashing car windows and taking what they can. What's interesting is that this is Ronin turf.

Quotes

"Yes, laddie. This ol' bit 'o sod the Ronins would be callin' their own, yes."

"Now, you wouldn't be denyin' some Leprechauns their hard-earned gold, would ye?"

"Well, *we* don't go around calling *you* names, do we? You're fine folk, and we accept that."

Notes

The Shamrocks are out for a stroll in Ronin turf. While they're at it, they've decided to help themselves to some pickings. They're not out for a fight, and won't try to start one. If hassled, they'll argue a bit, then move on to the next block, where they'll start over. If the runners follow, the gangers will get nasty, however.

The runners could fight the Shamrocks with their weapons, or they could let any Ronin contacts know about the Shamrocks' little stroll. The Ronins would owe the runners a big one.

Archetypes

Shamrock Leader: Use **Gang Member**, p. 39, **SR** rules, with Fichetti 500.

Typical Shamrock (5): Use **Gang Member**.

Info/Contacts

If the runners help out either gang, it will be remembered. The Shamrocks control their own piece of the Sprawl, and so the players could benefit from one or two contacts among them. The Ronins must be in trouble, judging by the way rival gangs are invading their turf.

The runners are relaxing, driving through Royal Reaper turf on their way to a bar or other likely entertainment spot. Suddenly, gunfire erupts around them as more than a dozen people on bikes roar out of an alley, firing at each other!

Quotes

"Get'cher bike from the Stuffer Shack?"

"Get off our turf, you drekhead!"

"You Ronins are gonna pay for this one!"

Notes

In response to the intrusions by the Royal Reapers and the Shamrocks, the Ronins have decided to have some fun. This crew of five are on their way back to their own turf after geeking the Reapers' King. Other crews are on the way to geek the Shamrocks' Leprechaun.

The runners' driver must make a Car Success Test to avoid all these bikes and the posts, buildings, and such on the side of the road. The Target Number is 6 for bikes and 8 for cars.

Archetypes

Ronins: Use **Gang Member**, p. 39, **SR** rules, with +2 on skills. Add Fichetti 500 pistols. One rides a Scorpion; the others have Rapiers.

Reapers: Use **Gang Member** riding a Rapier. One of the Reapers has an Ares Predator.

Info/Contacts

Either the Ronins or the Reapers need help, and will remember that help later on. On the other hand, the gangers will not so fondly remember some old fogey who hits their only Scorpion.

The distant sound of gunfire is in the air, and all smart chummers are safe in their beds. But since when have runners been that kind of "smart"? The gunfire is getting closer.

Quotes

"Outta the way, gramps! You don' move, you *dead*!"

"Geez! Geddouda my way, slugbrain!"

"You chummers see a hidey-hole 'round here?"

Notes

The gang-fighting in the Sprawl has finally been settled (for the month). The Ronins rumbled the Shamrocks, and geeked more than half the 'Rocks. Now the Shamrocks are running for home with the Ronins close behind. This could either be very good or very bad for the runners. If they are known allies of one gang, the others will either shoot to kill or avoid them, depending on whether they are the hunters or the prey. By morning, the Sprawl will be quiet again, until the Royal Reapers decide to claim most of the ex-Shamrock turf.

The runners meet Shamrocks looking to hide, looking to run, and trying to bargain for help. They'll also see victorious (and bloodthirsty) Ronins, drunk with victory but alert to any sign of trouble in their new turf.

Archetypes

Use standard **Gang Member**, p. 39, **SR**, for most combatants, with an occasional **Gang Boss**, p. 167, **SR**.

Info/Contacts

For a few months, the Ronins will have a stranglehold on any street activities in this zone of the Sprawl. You want to be on the street, chummer, you talk to them.

Up ahead, the runners see a table set up on the street. A crudely lettered sign is attached to the front, and a gang member is seated behind it. People are lined up before the table.

Quotes

"Breath tax? You pay, or you stop breathin'."

"Oh, a smart guy, huh? Well, look, gramps..."

"My pal Deadeye's on top o' the tower. Wave hello, Deadeye!"

Notes

The sign on the table reads, "Breath Tax. #25¥", but Elmo and Deadeye haven't thought through this scam. For example, what if the players' team shows up, or what about the Lone Star patrolman heading this way with blood in his eye? Deadeye, the friendly neighborhood Troll, is atop a nearby three-story building with a Remington 750 sporting rifle. Unfortunately, the thing's in such poor shape that all his Target Numbers are at +2. If the runners can let the Lone Star cop know that the sniper is

a Troll, he'll call for back-up before trying to deal with the two gangers.

Archetypes

Elmo: Use **Gang Member**, p. 39, **SR** rules.

Roscoe: Use **Gang Member**, with Troll Modifiers.

Lone Star Patrolman: Use **Street Cop**, p. 171, **SR**.

Info/Contacts

Many of the local citizens and businesses have paid this "tax." They will be grateful to "the guy who helped me out the time the hoods took my money."

The runners have been helping a store owner on Ronin turf. It seems that his stock of Hyper Krunch Cherry Crazie Sweeteez has been disappearing from his little grocery. At midnight, a desperate-looking girl comes banging on the door.

Quotes

"Please open up! They're coming!"

"Just hide me. Please!"

"Twenty minutes, mister! That's all. *Please*!"

Notes

Cherry is one of the younger girls riding with the Ronins. Somehow she didn't find out about a raid by the Barons until she saw some walking toward her. Unable to escape, she turned a corner and started to bang on doors. The runners are the first sign of life she's encountered. If the runners let her in, the Barons will assume she got away. If the timing is close, the Barons may start banging on the windows and doors, but won't be able to get in. (Isn't armored glass wonderful?)

If Cherry is still outside when the Barons show up, the gang will haul her off, laughing at her shrieks and screams for help. If the runners don't interfere, the Barons will take her back to their turf and initiate her into their gang, which is short of members). If Cherry ever meets the runners again, she may either blow them away for deserting her, or be glad she found a better home with the Barons.

Archetypes

Cherry: Use **Pedestrian**, p. 116, this book.

Barons: Use **Gang Member**, p. 39, **SR** rules.

Info/Contacts

If Cherry is hidden, she'll be a valuable contact with the Ronins. The current Daimyo, or gang boss, is her older brother.

The Cherry Crazie Sweeteez? The shop owner seems to be sleepwalking. (His wife put him on a diet.)

A truck moves through Baron turf, with a Jackrabbit behind and three Harley Scorpions in front. Punks in Ronin colors ride the Scorpions. A Ronin with an Uzi stands in a space cut through the roof on the Jackrabbit's passenger side.

Quotes

"Hoi, chummers. Nice night, eh?"

"We're just out for a ride. That's it, yeah."

"None o' your biz, chummer. Buzz!"

Notes

Warlock did just what the Ronins asked him to do. He busted into Megamedia's computer and got a shipment of simsense chips ready for pickup by the Ronins. Unfortunately, the truck is on Barons turf. The Ronins decided to move in, get the chips, and then take off as fast as they could, with all the firepower they could drag in. Now they're racing back to their own turf with a truckload full of the new simsense hit, "Waste Paper".

Nothing prevents the runners from trying to slot the truckload of chips for themselves. The Barons could also show up, wanting a piece of the pie. Whoever wins, they will end up feeling pretty stupid taking over a hot truck full of discarded paper. The simsense hit is entitled "Paper Trails." Warlock got the name wrong.

Archetypes

Ronin Guard Force: Use **Gang Member**, p. 39, **SR** rules, with Fichetti 500.

Barons: Use **Gang Member**.

Warlock: Use **Decker**, p. 34, **SR** rules, with PCD-100 Cyberdeck.

Info/Contacts

Either the Ronins or the Barons would be a good street contact, and the Ronins could help the runners get in touch with Warlock.

A gang of punks is headed down the street, looking for the runners, who haven't a clue as to why. As the punks approach, the player characters see that all have the same silly pouting look on their faces and funny little mustaches. They all look like wannabees of this old actor named…Chapman? Chapson? Something like that.

Quotes

"We will win. It is our destiny!"

"You will surrender and then you will die. You have no choice."

"Why are you attacking us? You can't beat us! YOU CAN'T! YOU CAN'T! YOU CAN'T!"

Notes

Meet the Ubermen, not a gang of Charlie Chaplin wanna-bees, but a gang of Hitler wannabees. They're out looking for revenge on the runners who geeked their leader, and they have mistaken the player characters for them. The Ubermen really don't care, so long as they get to kill someone. This is going to be a good old-fashioned slugfest any way you slice it.

Archetypes

Uberman: Use **Gang Boss**, p. 167, **SR** rules, with Retractable Spurs and Fichetti 500 pistols (re-cased to look like Lugers).

Info/Contacts

Ridding the plex of the Ubermen would be a boon to most of the local Mundanes. The gang has done nothing but disturb honest, hardworking people. Lone Star won't be crazy about having this mess dropped in their laps, but who cares what they think?

After a long night, the runners are heading back to their bikes. A cluster of Royal Reapers stands around one of the bikes. As the runners get nearer, they see that the lock on the bike's sidebag is broken.

Quotes

"This your bike, trog?"

"Think ya c'n rip off a Reaper, huh?"

"Laugh yer way outta cold steel, old man."

Notes

Earlier tonight, Acey-Deuce, a Reaper, ripped off the Reapers' stash of underground markers. When Jamon, the current King Reaper, found out, Acey-Deuce needed a place to hide the stash and a fall guy. He picked a runner's bike, then used a maglock passkey to open the lock. He hid the loot (including the maglock key) inside the bag, closed it, and claimed that he had seen the runner leaving the gang's HQ.

Jamon busted open the sidebag and found the stash. The runners cannot get out of this with firepower. If they geek the Reapers here, they'll be in a never-ending war with most of the city as a result. (Hey, only gangs geek gangs. Law o' the plex, chummer.)

It becomes apparent that the lock's delicate innerworks have been scrambled, as though someone used a maglock key on it. Now why would a runner need a maglock key to get into his own bag?

Jamon will realize that the runners are innocent. The next most likely suspect is Acey-Deuce. Say goodnight, Acey-Deuce.

Archetypes

Jamon: Use **Gang Boss**, p. 167, **SR** rules, with Elf modifiers and Ares Predator.

Acey-Deuce: Use **Gang Boss**, with Ares Predator.

Reapers: Use **Gang Member**, p. 39, **SR** rules.

Info/Contacts

Jamon is a power on the streets, and he knows (and is trusted by) a couple of the street's best fixers.

The runners have stumbled onto a stash of underground markers and ammo, mostly for light Streetline jobbies. As they are about to haul with it, a gang comes at them down the street. As they turn to head the other way, another gang approaches from that direction. Hope yer DocWagon's paid up, chummer.

Quotes

"Looky here, chummers. These old guys think they're gonna lift from a Ronin stash!"

"Hey, drekhead! That's not a Ronin stash. That stuff's ours! Fade, chummer!"

"Ronins put it here, Ronins take it! Not you drek-faced Rabid Rabbits!"

Notes

A few weeks ago, a Ronin scout found this stash on Royal Reaper turf, and removed it to Ronin turf. The Reapers scammed onto the location today. The Ronins, meanwhile, moved to save "their" find. Neither group is crazy about some troops of costumed old folks sitting on top of their stash.

This firefight could put plenty of holes in the players. If they move slow and easy, the gangs *might* let them out without the stash, but otherwise, it's lead city.

Archetypes

Gang Members: Use (Runners x 2) **Gang Members**, p. 39, **SR** rules, for each gang.

Ronin Boss, Daimyo Derek: Use **Gang Boss**, p. 167, **SR** rules, with an Ares Predator.

Royal Reaper Boss "King Jamon": Use **Gang Boss**, with Elf modifications and an Ares Predator.

Info/Contacts

Either gang is a great street contact, but King Jamon also knows a couple of "cooperative" fixers.

Five Shamrocks are walking down the street toward their bikes. The leader has a girl in Baron colors slung over her shoulder.

Quotes

"Top o' the mornin' to ya, gents. 'Scuse us."

"Now, why would ye be thinking that we're out o' place here, such foine gents like yersels?"

"She needs a lesson, and I can't teach her one here."

Notes

If Bonnie (the Shamrock leader) removes her hat, the runners will see that her head is bald. If pressed, Bonnie will admit that the Baron girl, Terry, poured Hyperwhisk Hair Remover into her favorite Strawberry Blond Super Mousse. Bonnie wants revenge for the loss of her waist-length hair.

She's won't release Terry until the other girl's red locks have been shorn, even after the local Baron contingent shows up. (Terry is their leader's little sister). If the runners can mediate, the best compromise is to have Terry's head sheared here, instead of on Shamrock turf. Duke (the Baron's leader) will argue for a while, but eventually agree to it as a just punishment.

Archetypes

Bonnie: Use **Gang Boss**, p. 167, **SR** rules, with Remington Roomsweeper.

Duke: Use **Gang Boss,** with Browning Max-Power.

Other Gang Members: Use **Gang Member**, p. 39, **SR.**

Info/Contacts

If the runners manage to get the gangs to talk instead of fight, Bonnie is a good street contact.

As the runners are leaving Lucky Luigi's Bar, a scowling young punker in Reaper colors approaches. As he draws near, the punker suddenly spins and drops, spurting blood. Then more gun shots ring out.

Quotes

"Get down! Sniper!"

"Hell! He geeked Freddie!"

"Come on! He's gotta run out of ammo sometime, and then he's *dead.*"

Notes

Brad, a Reaper, got dumped by his girl for another guy. Now he's decided to "slot the stick of the turf-taking jerk". Brad stole a semi-working Remington 750 and set up on the roof opposite Luigi's. He'll take potshots at anyone and anything that moves, and he's got a *lot* of ammo. Someone must take advantage of his reload time to head up there and stop him.

The Remington is in poor condition, with all target numbers at +2. Brad's back-up weapon (a Defiance T-250 shotgun) is dependable.

Archetypes

Brad: Use **Mechanic**, p. 168, **SR** rules. Substitute Firearms for Computer Theory.

Info/Contacts

Besides being a Reaper, Brad is a good mechanic. After this stunt, he'll *need* another job.

Most of the go-gangers drive Rapiers, a few are on Scorpions. The bikers' Mohawks extend to their waists.

Quotes

"Hey, chummer. Got a sec?"

"We're the Mohawks. Our turf is the entire Sprawl."

"We're always lookin' for good people."

Notes

The Mohawks care for two things in life; their bikes and their 'cuts. The bikes are maintained at peak condition, as are the Mohawks' long, flamboyant hairdos.

Josie, the leader, is a go-girl in her early 20s and the oldest member of the group. She of the flaming red hawk thinks one of the runners would make a good go-ganger. She will oversee his initiation by riding with the runner in any number of outrageous, daredevil stunts.

Archetypes

Josie: Use **Gang Boss**, p. 167, **SR** rules, with Bike 8 (Specialization: Scorpion) and a light machine gun (hidden) mounted on the bike itself.

Mohawk Member: Use **Gang Member**, p. 39, **SR,** with Bike 7 (Specialization: The model he/she rides).

Info/Contacts

The go-gang has excellent street contacts and hears about happenings all over the Sprawl.

Late one night, the runners are driving back home, when one of their bikes (or their car) hits someone. A second pedestrian manages to dodge out of the way. Both people look in sad shape.

Quotes

"They were holding us prisoner. Please help."

"I'm Jerry. He's Craig. We don't know this area, and they're on our tails!"

"They call themselves Libra."

Notes

Libra is one of the crazier gangs in the plex. They see themselves as the ultimate arbiters of justice and don't care who gets in their way. Most sararimen in the plex run for cover when the Libra bleeding Scales of Justice insignia appears. Most of the gangers ride Rapiers, use big guns, and wear body armor. The gang is made up of twins.

Jerry and Craig are also twin teens, down from the corp sector for a little action. When they smirked at a Libran pair, the gang imprisoned them. After five days, the boys escaped, then promptly got lost. They want the runners to take them to where a corp security group can take over.

Only eight Librans are on the boys' tail, but more are on the way. The ride uptown will take 80 minutes: 20 minutes for the trip, and an hour for the doc for Craig. Unless the runners keep to the shadows, 1D6 Librans will discover the group every 10 minutes. If the players' team gets into a firefight with Libra, 4D6 Librans appear after 10 minutes.

Archetypes

Jerry/Craig: Use **City Official**, p. 164, **SR** rules. Substitute Computer for Etiquette (Tribal).

Typical Libran: Use **Gang Member**, p. 39, **SR** rules, with Beretta 101T, Armor Vest with plates, and a Yamaha Rapier.

Libra Leader: Use **Gang Boss**, p. 167, **SR**. Ares Predator, Smartgun Link, Armor Jacket, Harley Scorpion.

Info/Contacts

Jerry and Craig know a couple of low-level corps, but the Librans have enemies up and down the plex.

Their Harleys bellowing and brilliant headlights strobing, Libra is on the prowl. From one end of the plex to the other, their Bleeding Scales of Justice insignia means death and destruction for "wrongdoers".

Quotes

"We are Libra. We balance the Scales of Justice with the blood of those who defile her."

"Up against the wall, punk! We know how to deal with *your* kind. Permanently."

"Get out of the way, cops! The defenders of Justice are legion. Will you really fight *her*?"

Notes

Libra is out for blood, for no one gets away with insulting them. Their prey are not the only ones who will suffer tonight, however. Anyone who crosses the street against the light, idly tosses a stuffer wrapper, or any other offense will merit only one punishment—Death.

The runners will initially meet a pair of Librans (identical twins). If the runners have done something illegal, the Librans will demand that they repair it, or else will open fire (calling for backup if there is more than one runner). The gangers will fight until the runner proves his superiority. At that point, the Librans pull back and call for back-up (if they haven't already).

Back-up arrives 2D6 minutes after the call goes out. It consists of 1D6 Libran pairs, with 1D6 – 4 Leader pairs (relatively rare). If the runners have fired on the Librans, they are "willful lawbreakers who must be destroyed."

Archetypes

Typical Libran: Use **Gang Member**, p. 39, **SR.** Beretta 101T, Armor Vest with plates, and a Yamaha Rapier.

Libra Leader: Use **Gang Boss**, p. 167, **SR**. Ares Predator, Smartgun Link, Armor Jacket, Harley Scorpion.

Info/Contacts

Libra has enemies up and down the plex. When fighting Libra, the runners will get help from many people, even those who would usually be enemies.

4

A runner is in his apartment, when a burst of automatic weapons fire tears through it. Donning armor and grabbing his HK227, he rips open the door to discover a girl on a Harley in the hall. She has a flaming red Mohawk down to her waist, and wears an armored synth-leather jacket. A smoking Uzi III sits on the Harley's gas tank.

Quotes

"'Bout time. Thought you moved faster than *that*."

"Ya didn't answer when I knocked or called."

"Hey don't worry! Pegs is housebroken." (Rides bike into living room.)

Notes

Josie is leader of the Mohawks biker gang. A hitman geeked her boyfriend today. She's taken care of the hitter, but wants the runner's help finding the man who hired him.

If the runner has contacts in the corp sector, he has heard that a certain corp wants to teach the Mohawks a lesson after a recent run-in. Josie may be getting more trouble than she bargained for.

Four of her gang are trailing her secretly in case she needs help.

Archetypes

Josie: Use **Gang Boss**, p. 167, **SR** rules, with Bike 8 (Specialization: Scorpion) and a light machine gun (hidden) mounted on the bike.

Mohawk Member: Use **Gang Member**, p. 39, **SR.** Bike 7 (Specialization: Whatever he/she rides).

Info/Contacts

Josie has street contacts and friends all across the plex, including several freelance security guards.

5

The runners have been sitting out in the rain for two hours, waiting for secret truckloads of a new Ares gun to go by. Here they come, but what are those bikers doing around the trucks?

Quotes (On wrist radio)

"Stalker One to Stalker Four. Check out unspecified disturbance. Quad 3ZED6."

"Stalker One to Mother Hen. E-T-A D-O-T (Dead On Time)."

"Buff One, Stalker One. Slot 'n run. Repeat, slot 'n run. (On loudspeaker). HEY, STALKERS! LET'S ROCK 'N ROLL."

Notes

The Stalkers, a little-known gang from the south end of the plex, made a deal with a local Ares Macrotech middle manager. Lone Star dealt themselves out of an escort job, and the Stalkers dealt themselves in, in exchange for much nuyen, new bikes, and big guns.

The corp has riggers running the four trucks (filled with dummy guns) from a remote location. They won't be risking Lone Star personnel on this decoy run. Just some minor street gang.

The Stalkers are riding close to the trucks, alert to danger. If they survive this encounter, they could probably develop into decent security guards. The twelve bikers are in standard guard formation: two in front, two behind, and one to either side of each truck.

Archetypes

Stalker Leader: Use **Gang Boss**, p. 67, **SR** rules, with Armor Jacket, Uzi III, Ares Predator, and Radio Headware.

Typical Stalker: Use **Gang Member**, p. 39, **SR** rules, with Lined Coat and a Colt America L36.

Info/Contacts

The Stalkers have some links into the local Ares branch, as well as street connections.

6

A screech of Yamahas is coming from the 25-story parking facility across the street. On about the 15th floor, bikes can be seen moving in circles, strobes lighting up the night. When (and if) the runners get up there, they'll see a young Mohawk being circled by six Libras.

Quotes

"Flaming scale-head! Whassa matter? You need better'n six to one before you attack?"

"You ain't Justice! Yer sickos who like to hurt people!"

"Make yer move, drekheads! 'N I'll take all o' you with me ta kingdom come!"

Notes

When the Libras started following this Mohawk earlier, he dodged into the parking garage, hoping to do a jump from the 3rd floor to the ground. Instead, the Librans forced him up to the 15th floor, then began to circle for the kill.

Because Mohawk Leader Josie recently insulted the Librans, they intend to reply by killing their victim. The other Mohawks are out looking for the boy, a fairly green member of the gang.

If the runners are having too easy a time with this one, feel free to produce Libra reinforcements. If they're having a rough time, introduce some Mohawks or Josie herself.

If the runners choose not to intervene, five minutes later a bike will come through the roof. (The captured Mohawk is more scared of Libra than he is of a long fall.) The gamemaster decides whether some miracle will let him survive.

Archetypes

Josie: Use **Gang Boss**, p. 167, **SR** rules, with Bike 8 (Specialization: Scorpion) and a light machine gun (hidden) mounted on the bike itself.

Mohawk Member: Use **Gang Member**, p. 39, **SR**, with Bike 7 (Specialization: Whatever he/she rides).

Captured Mohawk: Use **Gang Member**, with Wired Reflexes (2).

Libra Members: Use **Gang Member**, with Beretta 101T, Armor Vest with plates, and Yamaha Rapier.

Info/Contacts

Gangs are notorious for remembering both their friends and their enemies.

Smallish balding man, with a sour attitude. A wannabee shadowrunner.

Quotes

"Hey, chummer, you need back-up. I'm your man."

"Laugh now, you jokers, but regret later. I have friends, you know."

"'Smatter? You hotshots take it on the chin? No wonder, you dopes."

Notes

The bartender has wanted to get into the excitement of shadowrunning for longer than most folks have been alive. The runners have heard from some friends who once took the guy on a run that he panics easily and has all the subtlety of a sledgehammer. His one and only run ended in disaster.

Now he relieves his frustration by ratting on runners he hates. Having bugged several tables at his place, he hears plenty and passes it on to corp security.

Archetypes

Bartender: Use **Squatter**, p. 170, **SR** rules. Raise Charisma to 2.

Info/Contacts

This fellow knows a great deal about overt and covert activities in the neighborhood. He also has some security codes for RatNet, an informant network maintained by several corps.

If the players cross him, he will eventually make trouble for the group.

The waitress is pretty in a conventional way. Uses men and spits them out in the same way she seems to be perpetually chewing gum.

Quotes

"Don't pinch me, honey. I don't give free samples and you can't even afford to window shop."

"You're kinda cute. Ever thought of trying to make the *Guinness Book of World Records*?"

"Do me a favor, and maybe I'll do the same for you. Know what I mean?"

Notes

This girl is not used to being dumped by a man, so she's not too happy at the way her last conquest did just that. Little did he realize her vengeful nature or that he talks in his sleep.

A guard with a local *Zaibatsu* (Japanese megacorp), he mentioned an incoming shipment of chips for the corp computers. They are said to be coded for instant recognition by the corp mainframe, which drastically reduces IC torching time. With one of these chip monsters in his deck, a decker could skate through a corp's system virtually at will.

Archetypes

Waitress: Use **Bartender**, p. 163, **SR** rules. Reduce Sympathetic Listening to 3.

Corp Guard: Use **Corporate Security Guard**, p. 165, **SR** rules.

Info/Contacts

The waitress has dribs and drabs of rumor and dirt on everyone who hangs in the area. Most of her info consists of who goes out with whom and what each likes to do for pleasure. She also knows the favorite hang-outs for most folks.

If any player character rebuffs her advances, he can become the target of one of her future little plots.

The bouncer is a hulking Human brute who could pass for a Troll in the dark.

Quotes

"Izzatso? Mebbe youse wanna enlighten me outside, eh, chummer? Like now, right?"

"Dis ain't a hotel, chummer. You wanna sleep it off, hit the bricks. Now, or you'll fly in your sleep."

"Hey, I know this guy with some sharp software. Nasty skating stuff, waska? Wanna see?"

Notes

The Bouncer has killed his chances of ever having an original thought by drinking the rotgut brew his employer serves his patrons. The guy is earnest and can even be handy in a fight, but he's operating with many brain cells on the Injured-Reserve list.

While chucking out a drunk patron the other night, he snatched up an optical chip that fell from the man's pocket. Some half-crocked decker told him it was a smoking IC breaker. He's selling it for spit, but it will cut ice like no one's business (8-rated Sleaze program).

When used against the corp that created it, however, the chip will dump the decker's ID into a database for later reprisals.

Archetypes

Bouncer: Use **Corporate Security Guard**, p. 165, **SR** rules. Change Etiquette to Street, and drop Interrogation.

Info/Contacts

The bouncer knows things about local gangs, low-level corporate toughs, and the Yakuza. He's got some interesting stories about celebrities he claims to have tucked into a car after they got themselves wasted.

If the runners resist his sales pitch, he might be a tad rough the next time they get unruly in his joint.

The bartender is youngish and a good sort. Long hair and mechanical eyes. Slender, but no wimp.

Quotes

"Ain't that the truth? No matter how good we get with chips, men will never understand women."

"Jeezus, that's nasty, chummer. Here, have a shot of Red Eye on me. And they shot your dog, too?"

"Listen, chummer, that 'little lady' is a working girl on the CDC's Ten Most Wanted list. Got it?"

Notes

Chuck the Bartender is a nice guy, a rarity in the Sprawl. Besides his sympathetic ear, Chuck is an amateur fixer who puts together friends with friends. No runner who has him for a buddy goes hungry.

Chuck has a big problem, but he is not yet aware of it. Once he helped someone get work that resulted in a botched biolab run, and the runner has infected Chuck with a virus that is passed in sweat and breath/sneezes. It takes four weeks to incubate, during which time the victim is contagious. Chances are the characters are already infected.

A run on the lab will produce an antidote, perhaps in time to save Chuck, whose biochemistry reacts more gravely to this virus than does the normal Human's.

Archetypes

Chuck: Use **Bartender**, p. 163, **SR** rules.

Info/Contacts

This guy knows everyone and a little bit about everything. His info is low-grade, however. He's more than happy to share it, provided he gets quid pro quo from the runners. If Chuck isn't diagnosed and treated, however, he will die.

The waitress is a pretty, young redhead. She looks tired, with dark circles under her eyes.

Quotes

"Yeah, this is a service industry, but that means I hustle drinks, not customers."

"Can't meet you after work. I have to get home and take care of my kid."

"I need some help and I don't know where to turn."

Notes

She was married for all of six months about seven years ago. After getting her pregnant, the husband ended up in prison for pushing BTL chips. She divorced him and tried to escape by changing her name and moving to the Sprawl. She got this job two years ago and often mentions her son Donnie.

When her ex came out of jail, he located her and kidnapped the child. He believes she stole a cache of money he'd hidden, and he wants it back. (It was his partners who stole the money.) He has threatened to kill the child, and given her a deadline that is fast approaching. If the characters do not find the guy in 36 hours, Donnie will be history.

Archetypes

Waitress: Use **Corporate Secretary**, p. 165, **SR** rules. Remove the cyberware, set Essence at 6, change Etiquette to Street and Rumormill to General. Exchange Sympathetic Ear for Computer.

Ex: Use **Gang Boss**, p. 167. Carries an AK-97 and knows how to use it.

Info/Contacts

The waitress's son is a source of information. He tells his mother everything his schoolmates say about their parents. The data may have to be sifted for truth, but it will be good.

If the players refuse to help her, the waitress will probably kill her ex or herself.

The bouncer is a big guy, street samurai standard-issue. Black skin, gold eyes, and a knowing grin.

Quotes

"Let's step outside, chummer. We're out of sawdust, so you'll have to bleed in the street."

"D. is my middle initial. Give me enough nuyen and it stands for discreet. Ah, you are most generous."

"You talking about the new VP over there? I met him once. He's okay. Just likes the White Lady too much."

Notes

This Bouncer always has a story about this megastar or that corp type. It all sounds fantastic, yet his stories often turn up later in the scandal sheets.

He hires out regularly as a bodyguard/bouncer for elite get-togethers. His rep is solid and people trust him. A job coming up is a party to welcome a new corp type from Japan. Needing guys he can trust, the bouncer tries to recruit the characters. They will have to wear dress clothes and carry concealable popguns.

Roleplaying this scenario should be humorous rather than violent, as the runners attempt to fit in with society types. They might also make a good contact or two during the evening.

Archetypes

Bouncer: Use **Street Samurai**, p. 46, **SR** rules. Keep only the Fichetti Security 500. Needs Tres Chic clothes that allow for an Armor Vest beneath.

Info/Contacts

This guy really does know a lot of folks. His willingness to supply information is in direct proportion to how much he likes the runners and how much he hates the target.

If the players refuse his offer of work, he will never make them another or give them any help.

Normal-looking guy, dark hair and moustache. Has tan, but is nervous and ashen.

Quotes

"Watch it, buster. I'm a wiseguy. I got connections. La Familia, got it?"

"Outta my way, chummer, or you're fish food. The Don has me working. I don't need your lip."

"Hey, buddy, great to see ya. How's about helping a chum in a tight spot?"

Notes

This guy is a low-grade groupie with the local Mafia. He's not a made man, though he claims to be. The local Mafia tolerates him mainly because he is related to several important mob members.

Some of these relatives have been imprudent in their conversations around him. After he inadvertently passed on information about a heist to a police operative, the cops arrived and shot the local Don's son in the fray.

This guy desperately needs to get lost. He does have minor bits of useful information about the local Mafia, but he will not reveal that the mob is after him until after he's secured the player team's help.

If someone can get close enough to the Don to persuade him that the information leak was accidental, the Don might let this guy live.

Archetypes

Informant: Use **City Official**, p. 164, **SR** rules. Substitute Street for Tribal Etiquette. Arm with a Hold-out Pistol.

Mafia Soldier: Use **Mafia Soldier**, p. 113, this book.

Info/Contacts

This soldier knows much about the idiosyncrasies of the local Mafioso. He will, eventually, betray the players, by accident if not by design.

The Don's daughter is a black-haired, full-figured woman of intellectual and emotional passion.

Quotes

"No, I don't have anything planned for Friday evening. Concert? I'd love it."

"Some toughs are evicting the homeless from an abandoned tenement. Can you stop them?"

"I think I'm in love with you. God, if my father found out. Who is he? No one. I'm so happy…"

Notes

This woman is the daughter of the local Mafia Don. While in convent school, she learned who and what her father really was. She has since broken with her family, and attempts to make amends for her father's evil by working among the Sprawl's poor.

She has both charm and the strength to be tough when necessary. Falling for a shadowrunner was unanticipated, but she relishes the experience.

Her father has, of course, secretly been keeping tabs on her. He has curtailed his activities in the area where she works, but Dad has no patience for this romance with a runner. He has plans to snatch her off the street if the flame does not die out soon.

Archetypes

Don's Daughter: Use **Metahuman Rights Activist**, p. 169, **SR** rules. Raise Charisma to 4.

Mafia Don: Use **Mafia Don**, p. 112, this book.

Mafia Torpedoes (6): Use **Mafia Soldier**, p. 113, this book. SMGs and pistols for each.

Info/Contacts

Because the girl wants to forget her background, she will not openly reveal inside information about the Mafia family in the area. All she says are things like, "I heard X is in charge of vending machines," and so on.

If the characters alienate her, she will have nothing to do with them in the future.

The merchant is a normal guy, but with a haunted look. Disheveled and worried, unbathed and unkempt.

Quotes

"They nailed our cat to the door! They're animals. They said my kid was next! What am I gonna do?"

"Yeah, two ribs broken. They said it was a warning. My wife's taking the kids out of town."

"Waddayamean I don't need a gun. They're coming for me. I gotta do somethin', don't I? I ain't a wuss."

Notes

A long-time acquaintance of a runner has poured his life savings into a vending machine business. Starting with machines selling gum, candy, and drinks, he has finally begun to see some profits.

Because he started small, the vending machine Mafia missed his action at first. Now they demand 60 percent of his take, plus repayment of what they lost to his machines earlier. The local Mafia Don is willing to listen to reason. He's got torpedoes by the legion, but no wizzer runners. Swap out some service, no questions asked, and your friend will be "protected."

Archetypes

Helpless Merchant: Use **City Official**, p. 164, **SR** rules. Add a Hold-out Pistol.

Mafia Don: Use **Mafia Don**, p. 112, this book.

Mafia Soldiers (6): Use **Mafia Soldier**, p. 113, this book. Add SMGs and pistols for each.

Info/Contacts

This friend has a few connections on the legit side of the street. More important, his machines are fairly widespread. Disguised as a restocker or repairman for his equipment, a runner could get in almost anywhere.

If the players' team does not help him, they will soon hear that he died in a warehouse fire.

This collector is an Ork with beady eyes and mildew on his tusks. His attitude is as bad as his breath.

Quotes

"Da paper say you owe the yen. Pay the juice or we take it out of your hide."

"What loan? Don't give me dat, chummer. You counter-signed Ratface's note, remember?"

"I no lie. Look, here's your mark. So what, it's an 'X'? I know it's you 'cause Ratface said so 'fore he died."

Notes

Ratface, a vermin of your distant acquaintance, obtained a loan from a local shark. After non-payment, Ratface was geeked by the mob. One of the players' team is supposed to have countersigned the original note, but he never even saw it.

The collector's boss doesn't care who pays off the debt (20,000 nuyen, with 50 added daily for interest and penalties). The runner is a likely candidate because he is a runner with a decent rep.

The collector and his boss are vulnerable because they both skim the take. The collector's boss wants the runner to help him hide his assets from an audit by the Mafia Don. If the player character takes the job, he's off the hook for the loan, but runs the chance of angering the Don.

Archetypes

Collector: Use **Ork Mercenary**, p. 41, **SR** rules. Reduce weapons and armor to an Ares Predator.

Collector's Boss: Use **Bartender**, p. 163, **SR** rules.

If needed, use **Mafia Don** and **Soldiers** from previous encounter.

Info/Contacts

The Ork knows who owes what to whom. The player characters can buy paper (assume a debt) from him if they want leverage against someone in the future.

Unless the characters negotiate a solution, the debt will grow and the collector will turn it over to the Mafia Don for collection.

A typical Mafia soldier, pleasant but arrogant. Very content with his ties to his boss.

Quotes

"Me and Vinnie was out the other night. We met some trideo dancers and partied all night."

"Vinnie says I'm his Number 1 producer. That score off the Aztechnology shipment netted him 25,000 nuyen."

"Vinnie's my best chummer. I told him 'bout you guys. He wants a meet. Could be good stuff."

Notes

Vinnie is tied to a branch of the family on the losing end of a power struggle because the rival Don's hit crews are working overtime tonight.

Vinnie planned to bleed a rival mob's war chest by sponsoring a run into enemy territory. This is why he sent his loyal soldier out to find some runners. Vinnie gave up this information before he died, and now the rival gang's hitters are searching for his messenger.

The hitters will come on like gangbusters, putting the player characters smack in the middle of a Mafia civil war as they try to defend themselves. Their chances for survival are grim unless they can convince the Don of their innocence.

Archetypes

Low-Grade Torpedo: Use **Mafia Soldier**, p. 40, **SR**.

Hit Crew: Use **Former Company Man**, p. 37, **SR**.

Use the **Mafia Don** from **Encounter 2**, if needed.

Info/Contacts

The only thing this clown knows for sure is what score he has going down next.

If the runners refuse his offer publicly, the rival gang hitters might leave them alone. The Torpedo, however, does not want to fail Vinnie.

Tall, gangly, and wearing a 2,000-nuyen suit that almost shines. He hates it when people call him a dork.

Quotes

"Gentlemen, how foolish to believe you could hide this from *me*."

"We both know that you have it. Hand it over or I will arrange for some of Rocco's 'friends' to visit you."

"I do not negotiate. That I leave to Rocco and Shea. I like the way they...talk "

Notes

Richard, a low-level Mafia captain, somehow manages to work for two different gang families. With a turf war going on between his two "benefactors," he is in trouble. Fortunately for Richard, Vinnie died without fingering him. Vinnie, however, had a data chip with a copy of Richard's private diaries. Vinnie's messenger swears he gave the chip to some runners who hang out with one of Vinnie's boys.

Richard must get the datachip soon, or risk his Don finding out he's been getting rich by playing both sides of the fence.

The player characters don't know what he's talking about. The messenger wanted to get rid of the chip, so he slipped it to them without their knowledge. Of course, maybe Slick Mickey (the messenger) fingered the runners so he could keep the chip himself.

The Don already knows of Richard's little side jobs. If the characters get too involved with him, the Don may arrange for group rates at the local cemetery.

Archetypes

Low-Grade Captain: Use **Mafia Soldier**, p. 113, this book. Remove Unarmed Combat.

Rocco and Shea: Use **Corporate Security Guard**, p. 165, **SR**.

Info/Contacts

Richard is a lost cause in the information department. Nothing the characters do will please him.

About 30 local merchants are clustered around someone. Drawing closer, the runners see that they are surrounding a man dressed in a suit that would have been stylish five years ago. He's looking at a printout and reading off names. As each name is called, someone comes forward from the surrounding cluster to hand the man something. The speaker is outnumbered and seemingly unarmed, but it is his asudiene who look afraid.

Quotes

"Takashi-*san*, Lotus Rising Restaurant, 900 nuyen."

"Does anyone know where Miller-*san* went? You know how I hate house calls."

"You disappoint me, Theresa. I thought you knew better than to lie to me."

Notes

A little-known but no less ruthless Yakuza middleman, Andrew Musai handles three times the turf of a normal enforcer. He skims very little off the top, and is ferocious in his enforcement. One way he keeps people on their weekly loan payments is to make it a "roll call" where everyone can see how many people owe him.

Andrew will not deal with any runners who accost him, but will take their names and dispatch them later without being personally involved. He is civil at all times, and will never argue with anyone. No one toys with him for fear of what lies beneath his polite veneer.

Archetypes

Andrew Musai: Use **Company Man**, p. 164, **SR** rules.

Torpedoes: Use (Runners x 1.5) **Mafia Soldier**, p. 113, this book.

Bystander: Use **Pedestrian**, p. 116, this book.

Info/Contacts

Andrew has many valuable contacts on the streets as well as among the Yakuza. If it gets around that the runners have allied with him, many street people will no longer deal with them.

Two men and three women come out of a doorway further down the street. One woman is screaming and desperately trying to free herself from the grip of the two men.

Quotes

"Please! Somebody help me!"

"They're going to kill me! Please, I need help! They're going to—." (Slap!)

"Yo, chica. We're just going for a little drive, thas all."

Notes

The screaming girl is Laurie, a secretary at Bright Sky Inc., a Yakuza front organization. When she left Bright Sky two weeks ago, she took the keycodes to the company's bank accounts, worth several million nuyen. The Yaks put out a 250,000-nuyen bounty on her head. Her four captors are attempting to take her to Bright Sky for interrogation.

Laurie transferred the money from the corporate accounts onto a certified credstick worth 7.5 mil and hid it in her basement. She won't reveal the location because she's certain the Yaks will kill her afterward.

If the runners do not interfere, the girl will be hustled into a Toyota Elite and driven off. If the runners intervene, the two women will try to hold them off. When that fails, the two men will let go of Laurie and join in. At this point, Laurie takes off, and a general chase begins. None of the four are carrying automatic weapons.

Archetypes

Laurie: Use **Corp Secretary**, p. 165, **SR** rules.

Captors: Use **Street Samurai**, p. 46, **SR** rules.

Info/Contacts

Laurie will thank the runners profusely for their help, then promptly disappear.

A contact tells the runners about a locker in the monorail station that might contain a pleasant surprise, and he's right. They find a couple of HK227s, ammo, and several grenades in a gym bag. Too bad about the unpleasant surprise, however. Five men suddenly appear, surrounding the players and aiming their guns at them.

Quotes

"Greetings. I believe that you have something belonging to me and my associates."

"Perhaps you will be giving me the bag now?"

"*Domo arigato*." (Aside) "Kill them."

Notes

Tomoguchi-*san* recently bumped off his oyabun in an attempt to take the man's place in the Yakuza hierarchy. When another oyabun annexed the territory instead, Tomoguchi had to act fast before anyone could pin the murder on him. He stashed the murder weapons in a locker at the monorail station.

One of the men who helped him kill Asano recently changed sides and informed Kenor, Asano's successor, of the weapons' hiding place. Hearing this, Tomoguchi rushed to the station to remove the evidence. Seeing the runners removing his life from those lockers, he assumes that Kenor has sent them to steal the weapons.

Tomoguchi knows that Kenor will kill him once he has the evidence.

Archetypes

Tomoguchi: Use **Yakuza Boss**, p. 173, **SR** rules.

Kenor: Use **Yakuza Boss**.

Gunsels (4): Use **Corporate Security Guard**, p. 164, **SR**.

Info/Contacts

Tomoguchi and Kenor both have deep Yakuza connections.

The run was pure trouble from the start. The suits from Eagle had a Panzer marking time outside the building, security made the runners on the way in, and almost slotted their stick on the way out. When they finally got away, a patrol nabbed them three blocks from the building. While they're sitting in the clink, a guy comes to talk, and he's no suit.

Quotes

"Good afternoon. I have a business proposition to discuss with you."

"Let's just say that I am here to offer you an alibi, should you choose to accept it."

"*So ka.* You fear listening devices. Do not worry, none can work when I am nearby."

Notes

Before Kenshiro Kenor, a Yakuza oyabun, could create problems for a certain group of people, some runners did it for him. He is both mildly amused and pleased.

The runners were captured, and though they were indirectly helping Kenor, he cannot aid them without good reason. So he is here to make them an offer.

At the same time that the runners were making their run on Eagle, his people were engaged in similar activities not far away. With suitable editing of a few monitor tapes and with certain evidence planted here and there, he could clear the runners of the Eagle job. In exchange, he asks their promise to fulfill any request for service he might make in future.

If the runners refuse, Kenor will rely on blackmail to get their aid in the future.

Archetypes

Kenor: Use **Yakuza Boss**, p. 173, **SR** rules.

Info/Contacts

Kenor is familiar with most Yakuza and other underworld power structures and higher-ups.

A runner's customized Harley Scorpion blew up and took his girlfriend's Rapier with it. That relationship broke up real fast. The day is still going downhill.

Quotes

(Deadpan) "There's a bomb in my Sloppy Soy."

"What do you mean, DocWagon says I'm dead! I'm gonna be unless they come get me!"

"The last item on the menu says 'Death au gratin.' The way this day's been going, I'm *not* trying it."

Notes

A Yakuza hitman is on the runner's tail. Having studied his target for weeks, now he's ready to move in and neutralize the target, per instructions.

The hitman has a superiority complex that won't quit. He's cancelled the runner's DocWagon contract, and let the corps know that his SIN number is ready for reassignment. The runner will not have much problem realizing that someone is after him. The only questions are why and who.

The gamemaster decides why the Yak hitman is on the character's tail. Did the runner accidentally cross someone? Is he going out with some Yak's girl? Is someone trying to make a point? Or did someone make a mistake and finger the wrong runner?

In any case, between bombs in the most improbable places and accidents even Bugs Bunny never suffered, the runner will find it near impossible to conduct any business. He will also learn why he shells out so much money for DocWagon every year. That is, if he lives.

Archetypes

Yak Hitman: Use **Elven Hitman**, p. 166, **SR** rules.

Info/Contacts

The hitman can provide the runner with a Yakuza fixer contact if the runner is brave enough to call this guy and ask, "Why the hell are you trying to kill me?"

Half the people the runners know have been warning them away from this job, saying that it'll kill them. The other half reminds them how much it'll pay and that they have to look out for their reps. But someone else is calling them, and his kind of pressure isn't that easy to resist…

Quotes

"*Konnichi wa*, gentlemen. I am most anxious for you to proceed in a certain matter we both know of…"

"I do not think you are stupid."

"The choice is yours. You may act as I desire, or I will reveal your secrets."

Notes

Oyabun Indiri has reached into his files and come up with something in a runner's past so hideous that the runner cannot afford to have it revealed to the wrong people. Indiri would prefer not to use blackmail, but he has no choice.

He will try to treat the runners with respect. Though *gaijin* (non-Japanese), they are intelligent people.

Archetypes

Oyabun Indiri: Use **Yakuza Boss**, p. 173, **SR** rules.

Info/Contacts

This scene gives the gamemaster a chance to tailor the encounter to the specific plot of his game.

The runners are in their favorite hangout after a successful run, when a kid approaches. He has all the equipment of a runner, but it looks brand-new.

Quotes

"Hoi, gents. They tell me you're the best. I'd like to talk to you."

"I'm not so young. I'm 19. In our line of work, looking young can be an advantage."

"Tell you what. Try me. See if I'm as good as I say."

Notes

Roy Baker is the 15-year-old son of a local corp VP, but he decided to become a shadowrunner. Having purchased 100,000-nuyen worth of equipment, now he wants training.

He believes that he's shadowrunner material, and even has some useful skills. Between that and his equipment, he can be a useful ally. Of course, his father will not be pleased that his only son is becoming a runner, and the security boys he sends out won't like the fact that the runners kidnapped the VP's son. After all, he can't admit that the kid ran away.

Archetypes

Roy Baker: Use **Gang Member**, p. 39, **SR** rules. Subtract –2 on all skills.

Christopher Baker: Use **Company Man**, p. 164, **SR**.

Security Cops: Use **Corporate Security Guard**, p. 164, **SR** rules.

Info/Contacts

Roy knows how corporators think and act, and has so much equipment that someone could find just about anything he might need in Roy's stack.

A girl approaches the leader of the shadowrun team. She is in her late teens, dressed in synth-leather of an archaic style, and her hair is light blue with silver highlights. She chews gum vociferously, and she speaks with a "fifties carhop" accent.

Quotes

"Look, man. I got a propasishun for ya."

"My old man's Geoffrey Dugal. Like, maybe you heard of him?"

"Waal, I need, like, to drop outta sight. So daddyo can't find me."

Notes

Charity Dugal is the daughter of Geoffrey Dugal, an English nobleman who emigrated to the Sprawl to work with Walker Data Systems, the premier computer security firm. Charity, now known by her street name of Arrow, ran away from home with a street punk named Riggi. Mr. Dugal immediately called out

the cavalry, and now she's hunted wherever she goes.

Arrow would like the runners to arrange a false identity for her, after first arranging her "death" in an accident. She can pay them fairly well, though she isn't rich. Dear old dad, of course, *is* rich and might also be in the market.

Archetypes

Arrow: Use **Pedestrian**, p. 116, this book.

Riggi: Use **Gang Member**, p. 39, **SR** rules.

Geoffrey Dugal: Use **Mr. Johnson**, p. 170, **SR** rules.

Info/Contacts

Arrow knows quite a few younger "corp brats". Through them, she has claws into most of the corps. Riggi, a Royal Reaper, can call on 2D6 gangers for help.

A little old lady bustles up to you, pushing aside anyone in her way. She's got a duffel bag slung over her shoulder, and wears an absurd flowered hat.

Quotes

"I'm Kitty Cooper. My husband, soon to be ex-, is Rick Cooper. I want you to help me rip him off."

"I built Techtron with him from the ground up. Now he thinks I don't know about that floozie?"

"He's been embezzling money, hiding thousands of under-world markers in his office. I'm going to embezzle it back from him."

Notes

This little old lady remembers when Techtron was one little shop, instead of a chain of 34 stores. She and her husband worked hard, and it paid off. They're both in their mid 50s, and still going strong.

Six months ago, Richard Cooper removed his wife as vice-director of the company, and gave her a downtown store to manage. Three months ago, she began to guess that he was seeing another woman.

Something told her to take a look at the books, and she discovered hundreds of thousands of nuyen missing. Kitty intends to break into her husband's office to steal the under-world markers and bank account numbers. Because of her husband's poor memory, he's kept the same security codes for 31 years. Kitty is sure she knows them. She just wants back-up.

Play it up as best you can. Here's a little old lady opening a wall safe, throwing racks of markers into bags, and stumbling out with many heavy bags.

Archetypes

Kitty: Use **Fixer**, p. 167, **SR** rules.

Richard: Use **Fixer**, with –1 on all skills.

Info/Contacts

Kitty is a fun old lady, with contacts among many other people like her. She's perfectly willing to give helpful runners money, stock advice, or anything else that strikes her fancy.

It's the biggest party in town. No one knows who's paying, but it's free to all. Among the several thousand people in the hall, the runners spot a red-headed person that they recognize from the trideo.

Quotes

"Oh, migod. It's Sean Benton! I want his autograph!"

"What's Sean doing here? I never figured that he'd be here. Ya think he's paying for everything?"

"Probably. He's rich enough. Hey, what's that guy with the gun doing?"

Notes

Sean Benton is a champion Urban Brawl player. Having learned on the streets of the Sprawl, now he gets top nuyen from a corp. Despite his multimillion salary, he still has the heart of a street kid who misses his own kind. Every few months, he gives a party, with doors open to all. Benton usually goes unnoticed among the crush of so many guests.

Not this time, chummer. At this, the most wired party in the Sprawl, some gangers spot Sean. One of them is sure that Benton stole his girl, and he and his friends will make their move at the party. Suddenly pulling out their Fichetti 500s, they try to get close to Sean to shoot him. If the runners rescue him, the crowd will make them heroes, and it will certainly put them in Benton's good graces. Most fun he's had in ages. Now if they'll only take him along on a run...

Archetypes

Sean Benton: Use **Gang Boss**, p. 167, **SR**. Add Spurs.

Gang Members: Use **Gang Member**, p. 39, **SR** rules. Add Lined Coats and Fichetti 500s.

Info/Contacts

Sean is the reigning star of the Urban Brawl circuit and has many contacts in the sports world.

While heading home after a long night of partying, a runner realizes he's being followed. Almost at the same moment, shots whine off the wall near his head. From the sound, those are heavy slugs. Dodging between fragments of wall, the runner glimpses someone dressed in white and wearing a safari hat!

Quotes

"Drek! Missed him. Hand me another gun, Pete. This one's empty."

"He's lasted four minutes. Impressive, but I've seen better."

"Best hunt I've had in ages!"

Notes

Dale Winters used to be a famous safari leader in Africa before the tribes threw him and most other white men out. Everything else he tried—gaming, stock markets, mistresses, clubs for rich corpers—were boring.

While out for a walk one evening, a mugger attacked. After a brief scuffle, Winters killed the mugger. Looking at the man's dead form, Winters felt a warm glow and knew what he must do. He would safari again, but this time in the urban wilds of the Sprawl. And his prey would be man.

He and his three gun bearers are out hunting the runner. Between their hunting rifles and their rocket launchers, they're going to bag this prey.

Archetypes

Dale Winter: Use **Mercenary**, p. 40, **SR** rules. Add Sporting Rifle.

Bearers: Use **Street Cop**, p. 171, **SR** rules. Each has Sporting Rifle, with one missile launcher among them.

Info/Contacts

Dale is rich, and maintains contacts with many who specialize in the manufacture or sale of weapons.

Stacy Simpson, the well-known simsense starlet, has come to see one of the runners. If he's lucky, maybe she's looking for a co-star.

Quotes

"Hi, I'm Stacy. I'm sure you know me. I sure know *you*."

"You probably know me from *Vampires at Midnight*, my first hit. But I made one before that—a real dog appropriately titled *Bite of the Barghest*."

"I'd like you to talk to Tad Cross, who owns *Barghest*, and persuade him not to release that disaster."

Notes

Like any aspiring actress, Stacy worked at numerous other jobs before fame arrived. Besides jobs as a waitress, a singing telegram person, and a cabbie, she also made a little-known simsense "epic" under the name Vicki Menner. This low-budget, highly controversial "epic" is pure drek. Just knowing that it exists makes Stacy nervous.

The only ways to make Tad give up *Barghest* are (1) to persuade him that he will die otherwise, or (2) if he believes he can produce a new, higher-budget, and better-directed version. Ironically, Cross is in love with the divine Miss Simpson.

Archetypes

Stacy Simpson: Use **Simsense Star**, p. 50, **SR** rules.

Tad Cross: Use **Media Producer**, p. 169, **SR** rules.

Info/Contacts

Stacy and Tad both have contacts in the glitter world of simsense productions, but Tad's are earthier.

Tadashi is a distinguished Japanese gentleman of advancing years. Though the sedentary life is his style, he is alert to anything unusual. With bodyguard.

Quotes

"I seek certain information, which an acquaintance believes you can obtain."

"Perhaps you have heard about The Shark? Her security is said to be impenetrable."

"You claim to be the best. Can you be afraid of her?"

Notes

"Shark" is the street name of Fuyitama Ichikun, female CEO of Happy Memories, a local greeting data-fax firm. The older gentleman is Tadashi, her father and also director of Fuyitama Communications, owner of Happy Memories. Rumors that his daughter wishes to displace him have reached his Osaka office. He must put his suspicions to rest.

Not only is Ichikun beautiful, she is also a ruthless and skilled decker. Characters penetrating company security must still penetrate her personal security. Some will wish they'd stayed in bed.

The gamemaster decides the motivations of these characters. Is the Shark really seeking to replace her father? Are the Yaks in on it? And why does she hide behind a half-dozen bodyguards?

Archetypes

Fuyitama Tadashi: Use **Company Man**, p. 164, **SR**.

Fuyitama Ichikun: Use **Decker**, p. 34, **SR** rules. Change Etiquette to Street.

Bodyguards: Use **Bodyguard**, p. 97, this book.

Info/Contacts

Although he is a corp type, Tadashi values service well-rendered and might be willing at some later time to help a runner in trouble.

Hanging out at a bar one evening, the player characters encounter a young red-haired guy in new synth-leather clothing. Watching him from all over the bar are other men dressed in Urban Brawl gear.

Quotes

"Hi, I'm Sean Benton. Yeah, I know you've heard of me. Well, so have they."

"I need a favor. I came out here to relax, and now every wannabee in the city is following me."

"It'll be fun. What can go wrong?"

Notes

The hottest rookie on the Urban Brawl circuit, Benton has inspired a bigger wave of wannabees than anything since the Splatman simsense junkies all started thinking they were The Fool. The Urban Brawl championships begin in two days, and Benton's come down here to let off some steam. Somebody recognized him, however, and now he's trailing a good 40 Urban Brawl fans. Amazingly, one of the player characters looks so much like Sean that perhaps they could switch places so Benton can have some fun.

Some complications: Does Sean show in time for Sunday's game, or will the manager put the player character on the field instead? How will the disguised runner deal with the legions of adoring female fans? And what about the Yaks who want to make sure Sean throws the big game?

Archetypes

Sean: Use **Gang Boss**, p. 167, **SR** rules.

Warriors Manager: Use **City Official**, p. 164, **SR**.

Info/Contacts

This is a quick and dirty way for the runners to learn everything they did and did not want to know about organized professional sports.

Responding to female cries of distress, the runners find four over-chromed Arnie-Awesomes mugging a woman. Faced with superior firepower, the Arnies vanish into the night. To their surprise, the characters discover that the woman is "Aunt Sara," grandmotherly trideo idol of millions of fans of *Baking With Aunt Sara*. Imagine their further surprise when they discover that special makeup hides a beautiful young woman!

Quotes

"My goodness! Thank heaven you young folks happened along!"

"Aunt Sara always says there are nice people around. Tell me your names, and I'll send you a nice batch of cookies."

"Do you have any idea how big "Aunt Sara" merchandising is?" We're talking billions, boys."

Notes

Sally Hallock, the 28-year-old woman who portrays "Aunt Sara", is an up-and-comer with an eye on the profits. After being rescued by the runners, "Aunt Sara" will insist that they accompany her to a personal appearance. She won't take no for an answer, and the local scandal-faxes start scrambling for the "untold story" of Aunt Sara's relationship with the scruffy shadowrunners. How will the characters handle the media deluge? Or Aunt Sara's competition, who desperately want to destroy her reputation?

Archetypes

Aunt Sara: Use **Metahuman Rights Activist**, p. 169, **SR** rules. Substitute Cooking 6 for Leadership and Interrogation.

Arnie Awesomes: Use **Gang Member**, p. 39, **SR**.

Info/Contacts

If it's something involving the world of trideo, "Aunt Sara"' probably knows all about it.

An elderly man approaches the runners as they are relaxing one day in their favorite restaurant. Though his clothes are new, they're 40 years out of date. He asks for help.

Quotes

"Fifty years I've been keeping the kids of this town out of trouble. It just doesn't seem fair…"

"I'm sorry to disturb your dinners, sirs. It's just…Well, ya see, I need help and don't know where to turn."

"My boys are good, hard-working kids. No matter what they say, I can't believe Tony did it."

Notes

"Kris Kringle" was once the hottest decker to run the local Grid. For the past few years, Christian Heummer (his real name) has been running a decking "school" for some street kids. When his old nemesis, Colonel Warren Lourdes of Lone Star, learned of it, he put one of Kris's boys in the slammer. That's where the kid will stay, too, unless he spills the dope on Kris. Don't hold your breath, Colonel.

Not only does one of Kris's proteges need rescuing, but Kris wants to erase megapulses of files that Lourdes has on him. Lourdes keeps the files on a datachip not connected to the Grid. Kris won't let any of the characters, except maybe the decker, know his real identity. He says that the Lourdes datafile is incriminating to his kids.

Archetypes

Kris Kringle: Use **Decker**, p. 34, **SR** rules. Change deck to Fuchi Cyber-7.

Tony: Use **Squatter**, p. 170, **SR** rules. Double Attributes and add Computer 3.

Lourdes: Use **Company Man**, p. 164, **SR** rules.

Info/Contacts

Kris is a veteran of the local Grid and knows the location of more hidden back doors than perhaps anyone else in the Sprawl.

The characters are lucky enough to inhabit the same boarding house as Alex K. Stuart, Starmaker. He has the singular bad habit of constantly bragging about celebrities who owe him money. The characters have yet to see a star anywhere near him. Not, that is, until a celebrity turns up dead on Alex's kitchen floor.

Quotes

"Oh, my God! He's dead! I know he's dead!"

"Oh, why did this happen now, of all times? Sally Hallock is supposed to come over later. I'm ruined!"

"This never happened to me in Manhattan!"

Notes

Troy Mitchell is a small-time simsense star with a cult following. When he discovered last night that certain copies of *Lovers in Amber* were available as illegal simsense chips, he was livid. He protested loud and long to his bosses, saying he would spill it all to the press. Then he went to dine at his manager's house with his current paramour, Suzy Starbuck. Feeling the effects of a fine fettuccine Alfredo with a light garnish of cyanide, Troy asked for a Drop'N Fiz, but by then, it was too late.

This can be a fine lead-in to "Body, body, who's got the body?" as Sally Hallock ("Aunt Sara") shows up and Alex Stuart pleads with the characters to help him hide the body. And then there's the question of who tipped off the cops…

Archetypes

Alex Stuart: Use **Media Producer**, p. 169, **SR** rules, with no combat skills.

Suzy Starbuck: Use **Rocker**, p. 43, **SR** rules.

Sally Hallock: See **Celebrity Encounter 3**.

Info/Contacts

If the characters can pin this one on *anyone* besides Alex and Suzy, those two will be eternally grateful.

Street Season is being filmed on a runner's home turf, and they're looking for realistic extras.

Quotes

"You'll have fans screaming, ripping off your clothes…And you want money?"

"Not simsense fans, eh? Pay's O.K., and they're not difficult parts, and no trouble with the law."

"You know, we could use you for the big slam dance at the end of the program."

Notes

Stacy Starbuck, Suzy's sister, has problems. First, her drekky producer Marvin got caught peddling BTL chips, and now the Yaks want Jimmy (her new producer) to blow production so that he will be forced to default on loans they made to him.

How was Stacy to know all this when she co-signed the original loan? If *Street Season* gets made, she's clear. If not, she needs to find some protection, but she won't tell the characters that. If Jimmy doesn't comply, the Yaks intend to turn *Street Season* into their version of *Guadalcanal*. They have lucrative simsense projects in mind for Stacy, and aren't afraid to play hardball.

Archetypes

Stacy Starbuck: Use **Simsense Star**, p.117, this book.

Jimmy: Use **Media Producer**, p. 169, **SR** rules. Reduce skills/attributes 2 points each (minimum 1).

Info/Contacts

If the characters can save Stacy and Jimmy's skins, both will be ever grateful. Who knows, maybe one of the runners will turn out to be a decent actor.

Larry Ross is on the phone, and the semi-legendary star-maker has got such a deal for you.

Quotes

"Listen, kiddo. When L. Ross says something is a great idea, don't argue. Am I right?"

"It's your chance to fight the corps in the only arena where you can really beat them."

"Prime-time Tri-V! With Jermaine himself!"

Notes

Ratings week is coming up for Jermaine Jerard's celebrated talk show, *Heavy Hitters.* The once-top-rated show has recently slipped to number two, and Jermaine has an idea. A debate show between a group of corpers and a group of shadowrunners! The corporators:

Karen King of Ares, an attractive, no-nonsense security type. Relatively well-disposed toward runners.

Terry Newell, the elderly CEO of Eagle Security. A fierce anti-runner.

Isoroku Mesatiri, aggressive young CEO of the Sprawl's Fuchifax, often employs runners.

Ichikun Fuyitama, the "Shark," CEO of Happy Memories and violent enemy of Mesatiri and any runner.

Visible weapons will be checked at the door, but most of the corps will carry hidden arms.

Archetypes

Larry Ross: Use **Fixer**, p. 167, **SR** rules. Add +2 on all skills.

Jermaine: Use **Bodyguard**, p. 97, this book.

Karen King: Use **Bounty Hunter**, p. 163, **SR** rules. No cyberarm.

Terry Newell: Use **Fixer**.

Mesatiri: Use **Mr. Johnson**, p. 170, **SR** rules.

"Shark": Use **Decker**, p. 34, **SR** rules. Change Etiquette to Street.

Info/Contacts

Jermaine Jerard and Larry Ross have extensive contacts in the media world, while most of the corp types pull major clout in their own sphere.

An old friend in the tri-vid business contacts a shadowrunner with a proposition.

Quotes

"Peter Duran has the highest-rated sleuth-show on the air."

"He wants to explore the perils and plusses of running."

"I thought you might like the chance to be famous, to tell the 'Sprawl scum' side of the story."

Notes

Peter Duran is an investigative reporter who wants to explore why runners exist. He'd like to accompany a team on a mission and talk to them about why they've chosen this life.

He's not a runner, but he can keep his head down, hide, and shoot with the best of them. With his mini-recorder and mini-cam, he won't need a crew. And finally, the people will *know.*

It's liable to turn messy, with the corps trying to squelch Duran and his story, but the free press goes on.

Archetypes

Peter: Use **Rocker**, p. 43, **SR** rules. Some armor.

Info/Contacts

Peter shows up in the most unlikely places. Today, he may be investigating megasleaze in the rocker world, tomorrow corruption in the financial community. A ferret for a great story, he always protects his sources.

Word on the street is that someone wants to meet with the team's decker and is talking six figures. When the decker shows, the contact is a girl in greasy coveralls, probably some poor wage slave with delusions.

Quotes

"Wait. I know what I'm talking about."

"What would you say if I said 250,000 nuyen?"

"It'll take guts. I hear Warlock's better than you, and has more guts. Convince me."

Notes

Erica Farrell was fired from the support staff of the trid game show, *Lucky Lady.* With the show's computer randomly throwing out sparks, they're only starting to realize how much they miss her. Erica and her two accomplices intend to become the Luckiest Ladies of all time by reprogramming the computer. All they need is a decker for their master plot.

The plan is Erica's, the codes for accessing the computer are Tracy's (also fired), and Marie is set as a contestant on the show.

Lucky Lady is based on the card game Blackjack, except that the computer generates the cards. Erica wants the decker to rewrite some of the master game program code to favor Marie.

A program is mighty complex, however. What if the decker doesn't successfully change all the code? "I have three Queens... of Spades?" What if a corp decker figures out what is going on and starts a fight? "Gee, the cards are blinking on and off and changing." What if the runners find out that the ladies don't plan to pay them?

Go for it, gamemaster. The cards are hot tonight. Before the night's over, the world of game shows will never be the same.

Archetypes

Erica: Use **Dwarf Technician,** p. 166, **SR** rules, without racial modifiers.

Tracy: Use **Media Producer**, p. 168, **SR** rules.

Marie: Use **Corporate Secretary**, p. 165, **SR** rules.

Info/Contacts

The Terrible Three know the technicians from most of the top-rated trid shows, and could probably arrange almost any meeting the players need to make with media techno-types.

Word in the Sprawl is that some angel is out and about, asking questions and generally playing the busybody. Unfortunately, she found you.

Quotes

"But I'd just like to talk to you. . ."

"Oh, please, what can it hurt?"

"Look, chummer! I just want to ask a coupla fraggin' questions about the Sprawl, O.K.?" (Quieter) "I thought so."

Notes

Kerry Taylor is famous for human-rights reporting. She broke the story on the Quanatico Elven slavery ring, proving that there was official involvement. She talked with refugees of the corp wars in Africa. Now she's on the home front, wanting to publicize the desperate plight of the poor who have fallen in between the corporate cracks. It won't be that easy, however. To quote Black Ike, "She's gonna blow in, get her ratings, then blow out with another million-nuyen 'exclusive.' But we gotta live here."

The only thing that will stop her from telling too much about the Yaks, the Mafia, and other general corruption is if someone kills her first. She'll probably make it through, but in what shape?

Archetypes

Kerry Taylor: Use **Former Wage Mage** (Healer Orientation) p. 38, **SR** rules.

Info/Contacts

Kerry has some magical contacts, though she's careful to keep those under wraps. She can offer the player characters connections to other socially concerned people, and would surely help them if needed.

A player character is relaxing after a hard run, when floodlights suddenly flare on. As his cybereyes compensate, he sees a complete film crew, all wearing *Tech Trak Tonite* sweat-shirts!

Quotes

"Hell. Get some dulling spray on that cyberarm!"

"What do you think of the new HK227SE? Haven't seen it yet? Well, here!"

"Watch the wires, spaz!"

Notes

Tech Trak Tonite is a popular trid show that reviews street hardware, plays with it, and raves over it, no matter how good or bad. One of their favorite stunts is to corner some poor street samurai and start interrogating him. "You just stole the super-secret such-and-such from such-and-such corporation. Are you using it yourself? What's it like? Was it worth it?"

Hey, it won't all be for naught. The runner will get a "TTT" sweatshirt.

Archetypes

Harlan Hayes (producer): Use **Media Producer**, p. 169, **SR** rules. Substitute Estimate Value of High-Tech Items for Etiquette (Corporate).

Techs: Use **Dwarven Technician**, p. 166, **SR** rules. Subtract 2 from all skills. Add Firearms 3.

Info/Contacts

The *Tech Trak Tonite* people are understanding souls, with contacts among the mercenary and samurai circles as well as among most weapons corps.

In the last six hours, no one has answered or returned any of the runners' business calls. Then the bartender at Lucky Luigi's Bar calls to ask them to come down for a meet.

Quotes

"Surprise!"

"Congratulations!"

"How does it feel?"

Notes

It may take the runners some time to figure out what's going on, because the crowd at Luigi's seems to think they already know.

Present is Mr. Timothy Reardon, the somewhat infamous publisher of the annual *Who's Who on the Streets*.

With great fanfare, he announces that the players' team has won the award as this year's best shadowrunners in the Sprawl. With this, the festivities rise to a new pitch, with a good time had by all.

Archetypes

Timothy Reardon: Use **Media Producer**, p. 169, **SR**.

Info/Contacts

Reardon knows the international media scene, and also some of the best runners around.

Dressed in skin-tight synth-leather and sporting Good As Gold on her neck and each wrist, this corp secretary is far from typical. She likes to drop by to see one of the runners now and then.

Quotes

"I'm not sure. I'm only Mort's secretary, but—"

"Gossip says that Murray's about to push, in a big way."

"LaVerne's boss just commissioned a run on Techtron to get even for them wasting the new transmission tower."

Notes

Abigail is a secretary for Mort Powell, a mid-level corp exec. Sitting outside his office, she hears a lot, not to mention tidbits she hears the other secretaries discuss. She keeps up on what's happening. After all, a girl's gotta have something in the bag, doesn't she?

Abby is a good contact. Runners who treat her well may get a warning of when security's about to drop in or perhaps learn of a corp file on a potential enemy. A secretary can accomplish much, especially when she has a corp-authorized copy of her boss's credstick.

Abby's only weakness is a craving for real chocolate. To get as much as she needs means buying through the black market.

Archetypes

Abigail: Use **Corporate Secretary**, p. 165, **SR**.

Mort: Use **Corporate Official**, p. 107, this book.

Info/Contacts

Abby is a competent secretary, indispensable because she knows more about what's going on than Mort does.

A homely guy in his late 50s, Ed wears coveralls and an old Supersonics baseball cap.

Quotes

"Let's see…I been runnin' this loading dock for, oh, twenny years."

"Every so often someone in shipping makes…mistakes…I'd guess you'd call 'em."

"Well, I gotta get rid of them before inventory finds out, and you could use something like that, so—"

Notes

Ed Murphy has worked on the loading dock so long he almost feels like he owns it. What he's doing isn't stealing. Not by a long shot, no sir!

He's just spreading the wealth around. Besides, the corp's insured for losses and those lazy suits don't care about anything except sitting at their fancy desks and giving orders.

Archetypes

Ed: Use **Humanis Policlub Member**, p. 168, **SR** rules. Change Demolitions to Negotiation.

Loading Dock Worker: Use **Dock Worker**, p. 109, this book.

Info/Contacts

Depending on what shipping decides to screw up this month, Ed can get the runners almost anything at about 50 percent of normal prices. Depending on how restricted the stuff is, this might work out to as little as 1 percent of street prices, however.

Across the table is a fat man in his mid-30s. From the look of him, he's a low-level suit who'll never go any higher. He's not even bright enough to take off his 15-year corp service pin in the middle of gang turf.

Quotes

"Hello, I'm Elliot…er…Mr Johnson."

"But aren't markers illeg—? Oh, yes. Right. Markers. I'll pay with a certified credstick."

"You'll have to forgive me. I'm really not too good at this sort of thing. You see, it's my first time."

Notes

Elliot Barker is assistant district manager of the local Stuffer Shack franchise. He's somewhat addicted to Sweeteez, and looks it. His wife has persuaded him that the only way he can rise up the corp ladder is if "something happens to Eric (Elliot's boss)."

Now Elliot is trying to find someone to do a run on the local Stuffer Shack when Eric is inspecting. Not to kill him, but just to hurt him and put the fear of God into him. Though he can't afford to pay now, Elliot will give the players twice what they're asking, once he's district manager. He can also get them anything they want from the Stuffer Shack.

Michelle has different ideas. She wants Eric dead, no matter how it happens. If she's lucky, Eric will get geeked in the shuffle.

Archetypes

Elliot: Use **Mr. Johnson**, p. 170, **SR** rules. Delete cyberware and subtract 2 from all skills.

Michelle: Use **Mr. Johnson**. No cyberware.

Eric: Use **Company Man**, p. 164, **SR** rules, with Remington Roomsweeper.

Info/Contacts

Elliot is both naive and sincere. A district manager at Stuffer Shack is a nice friend to have and a good source of street gossip.

Standing across from you is a big guy in his late 20s, wearing what looks like an expensive real leather jacket and some old-fashioned denim jeans.

Quotes

"Wyn Carver. Perhaps you've heard of me?"

"I'd like to do a field test of my new device."

"I would never do a thing like that. My devices are safe. That's how I build them."

Notes

Wyn Carver is a young inventor with Tagmatic, a subdivision of Ares Arms, which is a subdivision of Ares Macrotechnology, which is a subdivision of…oh well, you get the idea. He has a new invention, and doesn't want to wait for the request to travel up and down the corp ladder before he can test it. He needs a band of intrepid runners to do it for him.

Wyn's new Smart Goggles are designed to let the wearer operate a gun in each hand simultaneously. They work by using a separate targeting sight for each gun. Because of the distracting effect of the two sights, all Target Numbers are at +2, instead of the normal –1 for Smart Goggles.

Archetypes

Wyn Carver: Use **Decker**, p. 34, **SR** rules.

Info/Contacts

Wyn has a pipeline (however slow to respond) into Ares Macrotech, and contacts with many other inventors.

Unable to unearth the information necessary to their current mission, the runners have gathered to discuss further options. Suddenly, the phone rings.

Quotes

"Good evening, gentlemen, my name is Patron."

"I understand you need some information. If I might be permitted to suggest an avenue of investigation…"

"I know many things. Only one of them is the place of your meeting tonight."

Notes

Patron is an enigma, a corp exec with a taste for mystery and the power to indulge it. He will provide the runners with a way to obtain the missing info, and can be used as a deus ex machina if the runners completely miss a connection. Patron does not stress it, but his connections are probably superior to those of the player characters.

Patron should remain a shadowy figure for some time, and is best kept a mystery. At some time in the future, he may call upon the characters for help, or once again aid them in some other way.

His real identity? He could be male or female, Human or Troll, even a computer program. Voiceprint analysis won't reveal anything about him, even if the runners think of doing one.

Why does he help the runners? Perhaps a sense of justice, perhaps a vicarious thrill. Who knows? The gamemaster decides.

Archetypes

Patron: Use **Company Man**, p. 164, **SR** rules.

Info/Contacts

The runners can never call Patron. He will always call them. Because of his presumed resources, consider his information sources those of any corporate executive.

The runners are in a bit of trouble. It's not the four *shaikujin* from Eagle Security, but the patrol vehicle carrying three other cops that's the problem. Those three can fire out through gunports, and the runners can't hit them. Suddenly, an AVM rockets through the air from a nearby Westwind, hitting the patrol vehicle!

Quotes

"Lock 'n load, lil' darling."

"No prob. They're gone."

"Ain't lookin' for nothin' but a good time."

Notes

Sidewinder's a corp rigger with a mischievous streak a kilometer long. He likes to drive corp security suits crazy, and this is his favorite way to do it. In his spare time between jobs, he helps out runners.

Sidewinder is something of a legend on the streets, and most street folk respect him. Between his rigged Westwind and his corp connections, he usually comes off as a god-like being, showing up as an ace in the hole just when all looks hopeless for some runners.

Archetypes

Sidewinder: Use **Corporate Rigger**, p. 107, this book.

Info/Contacts

The runners can contact Sidewinder via message drops and other assorted means, but they never see him physically. He shows gleeful delight at foiling the aims of any security folk, and may have information relating to riggers or corporate folk.

In the middle of an evening's relaxation, one player character notices a familiar woman sitting across the dance floor. Not familiar-friendly, but familiar little-warning-bells. As he watches, the girl slowly stands and janders across the floor. Reaching the characters' table, she pulls out an Ares Predator in a lightning-quick draw.

Quotes

Nobody moves! Nobody gets hurt!"

"Don't try scamming me! Back-ups are already on the way! You move anything, I put a hole in it!"

"You sewer rats thinks you can rip off Fuyitama and get away with it! Not with Ann McQuarry on the job!"

Notes

Meet Ann McQuarry, one of the newest recruits for Fuyitama Security Endeavors, special security agency for the team's favorite or least favorite corp. Just out of her six-week training course, she's green as grass. She believes the characters pulled off a heist on one of the corps that Fuyitama guards. She's been following them all evening, and even remembered to call for back-up.

The Fuyitama training course is six weeks of high-intensity information overload, so she could be wrong. Maybe she only saw these runners on some security camera tape. Or maybe the characters are guilty but can find a way to confuse the neophyte security cop. Or, the real guilty parties may be hanging out in the same club, and are starting to feel real insecure.

Archetypes

Ann McQuarry: Use **Street Cop**, p. 171, **SR** rules. Arm with Ares Predator.

Info/Contacts:

Once this all gets straightened out, Ann could be a worthy contact. She is intelligent, perceptive, and trustworthy, and will be good at her job once she has more experience.

A tall, physically monstrous Lone Star cop wearing heavy body armor and carrying tons of firepower struts up, almost reeking self-satisfaction and derring-do.

Quotes

"Well, boys, having a little party, are we? You know how we feel about street punks having parties without a license, don't ya?"

"Well, I'm not sure if a certified credstick for 500 nuyen qualifies as the right paperwork. Seems more like bribery to me."

"Seems to me that really bright punks like yerselves would know better than to insult an officer of the law."

Notes:

At Lone Star Security, there's nobody better than "Wild Bob Monroe." (Just ask him.)

Wild Bob has the day off and really wants to bust some heads. Armed with his gen-u-ine (non-working) H&K 207 and his gen-u-ine antique (working) Ruger Super Blackhawk, he's on the prowl for street trash. (Unfortunately, his gen-u-ine ex-wife had the courts repossess his antique Harley after he missed five alimony payments to buy a rebuilt carburetor for the bike.)

He's hopped the monorail downtown and dearly wants someone to insult him.

Archetypes

Wild Bob: Use **Merc**, p. 40, **SR** rules. No gear, except for Armor Clothing and Ruger Super Warhawk.

Info/Contacts

Wild Bob claims to know much about the inner workings of Lone Star, but that is not the case.

It was bad when someone surprised the team's decker in the real world and shot his deck full of holes. It got worse real fast when someone locked onto another runner's "Macho Mod" Westwind and blew it to bits with an AVM. Now some suit's on the telecom, and he says he knows what's flying.

Quotes

"You sewer scum thought you'd slotted me for good, didn't you? Well, William J. Russel isn't that easy!"

"They say enough nuyen will buy anything. It's true. Good luck, chummers."

(Telephone Operator) "I'm sorry, but the number you have reached has been obliterated. If you have any further system problems, please call…"

Notes

William J. Russel used to be an honest (well, semi-honest) security officer, until the players disgraced him on a previous run and he lost his job. Russel is only alive because a doctor replaced 90 percent of his body with cyberware. Now he wants vengeance. With plenty of nuyen in his hidden Denver bank account, he has hired several mercs with enough firepower to turn the Pacific Ocean into sushi.

Between Russel, his mercs, and assorted armaments, the characters are in for a rough time. Even if they win, it will only be by calling on every resource at their command.

Archetypes

Bill Russel: Use **Street Samurai**, p. 46, **SR** rules. Change Etiquette to Corporate.

Info/Contacts

Russel gets his money through an illegal conduit into a former employer's pension fund. Should the corp learn of this, they would certainly assist the characters.

A petite, good-looking woman contacts the characters. As they sit down to meet with her, one runner notices she has a concealed Roomsweeper.

Quotes

"Don't worry. I've looked at your records, but your crimes don't interest me. Your resourcefulness and cunning do."

"I'm a 'corper' and you're 'punkers'. I don't think either of us can afford to be seen with the other."

"I think we've got some 'slushers' out there, and I don't like crooks taking the nutrisoy out of honest people's hands."

Notes:

Young Diana Berg is the competent Assistant Security Director for her company. The problem is her extreme concern for her fellow employees, which can be bad for business. She has seen internal reports indicating that some of the most trusted warehouse supervisors may be "slushing" money on the side.

Actually, the gang, which includes most of the warehouse personnel and eight security men, has been operating for the last seven years, lifting a minimum million nuyen per year. Because the leaders are trusted workers and guards on the busiest daytime shifts, the gang can move the "slush" during the times of heaviest activity, allowing them to camouflage their steal.

Oh yeah, the ringleader? He's Diana's boss.

Archetypes

Diana Berg: Use **Company Man**, p. 164, **SR** rules. Add Armor Vest and Remington Roomsweeper.

Info/Contacts

Except for the executive suites, Diana has keycode and palm-access clearance to all sections of the corporate HQ.

A contact calls.

Quotes

"Me? I'm taking a vacation. I'm not stupid."

"I know you and you know that you didn't do a run on Happy Memories. But who's gonna tell *them*?"

"Tomcat says the order just went out. Pick you all up. Ice breaking."

Notes:

Every shadowrunner's deepest nightmare: corp types with a mind to pour you into the support columns of the new monorail line. Tomcat, a decker, just picked up an order in the Happy Memories, Inc. databanks calling for its cops to pick up the characters for industrial espionage. The order further authorized termination if the runners tried to escape capture.

The runners have been framed by Ace Mitchell, one of the corp's own security men, who has been leaking Happy Memo-

ries' new slogans to a competitor. To save his own skin, Ace pointed to a dossier on the characters that happened to be lying there when the Shark (company CEO) stormed in to demand some answers.

Archetypes

Shark: Use **Decker**, p. 34, **SR** rules.

"Ace": Use **Company Man**, p. 164, **SR** rules.

Happy Memories Security: Use **Corporate Security Guard**, p. 165 **SR** rules, with Armor Jackets and Uzi IIIs.

Info/Contacts

Most of the runners' friends are going to be busy protecting their collective tails right now. There may be a dataslave from Happy Memories or its competitor, Fuchifax, who can either find the leak in Happy Memories' security or in Fuchifax's payroll records.

In the midst of a tough run, alarms begin to howl and computers go on guard. Obviously, someone sold the runners out. Big mistake for them.

Quotes

"I am a man of integrity as well as a corper."

"I cannot be bribed, at least not unless you offer more money than I get now."

"I have bills to pay. Is there any law against working for more than one employer?"

Notes

A contact managed to get Ares Macro's Alpha Strike Blue keycodes, which govern physical and Matrix access. Alpha Strike Blue is a high-level executive passcode that would make With Mulholland Point's hard storage in their hands, the runners could blackmail Ares for all it's worth.

When the decker is halfway through Ares security during the run, the door just ahead starts to flash: "ALPHA STRIKE BLUE COMPROMISED. USE ALTERNATE PASSCODE WITH THUMB-PRINT CONFIRMATION." The team has been sold out, and Ares knows they're at Mulholland. They couldn't put this kind of security on every installation or it would shut the whole corp down.

With corpers all over the place, the first step is survival. Next, get out alive. The third is revenge.

If the decker is smart, he'll have used the AS-Blue codes to get into the storage area to start lifting other passcodes and data. Though Ares Security prevents anyone from learning any other complete passcode except for the one they are using (AS-Blue), he may be able to get partial codes.

Archetypes

Ares Security Guard: Use **Corporate Security Guard**, p. 165, **SR** rules. Armor Jacket and FN HAR.

Info/Contacts

The team's decker may think to start downloading data into his deck from the master storage units. He probably won't be able to get much before the keycode is cancelled, but it'll help pay for the ammo used.

One of the runners gets a call from a friend. The friend sounds very scared, and it doesn't take an Einstein to figure out why.

Quotes

"I'm telling you! It's the Knight!"

"I know Swift killed him. But he's back!"

"He wants Swift, and doesn't care who's in the way!"

Notes

The Urban Knight is a legend among corp cops, and well-known among runners. With his rep for deadly accuracy with his Predator, some whispered that he could not die. An expert in weapons, tactics, and explosives, the Knight flew a Federated-Boeing Shadowraith chopper in the corp wars and brought it back home when transferred. Three weeks ago, an Elf samurai named Swift killed the Knight. Five witnesses swear that Swift threw Knight into a giant turbine at the hydroelectric plant.

But someone dressed in the Knight's spectacular blue and silver body armor is loose in town, with enough firepower to sink a battleship. He wants Swift.

Could this be Knight? They say really powerful wizards can do anything, but it ain't possible for someone to come back from the dead. Or is it?

Archetypes

Knight: Use **Bounty Hunter**, p. 163, **SR** rules, with full Heavy Armor.

Swift: Use **Elven Hitman**, p. 166, **SR** rules.

Info/Contacts

If the runners find Swift through a contact, he will inform them that the Knight is definitely dead, and then arrange for some backup. This is a chance for the gamemaster to throw in anyone or anything he's been wanting to introduce or thinks the runners should have.

The runners are heading home for the evening. As one unlocks his door, he hears a distinctive "click" followed by a huge explosion that knocks the nearest runner down. Emerging from the dust of the explosion is a massive form, with another to either side.

Quotes

"Hoi, chummers. Hold on a mo'."

"Yer not good enough for the heavy guys, so they sent me."

"Do yer want's to go quiet or real fun-like?"

Notes

Over time, the runners have managed to avoid the best the corps could throw at them. They've shown up security forces, splattered samurai, and dumped the best deckers money could buy. They've finally gotten the corps angry enough to finance a run against *them*.

The corps have called on an experienced team named the Mean Machine. These four mercs have traveled all over the world doing in other runners. Now they're back to do their bit in the runners' town.

The decker will be jacked in, monitoring the building's security and housekeeping devices. The three in the doorway are a Troll flanked by a Dwarf and an Elf. Standing by outside is a fall-back force consisting of standard security officers.

Archetypes

Human: Use **Corporate Decker**, p. 106, this book.

Elf: Use **Elven Hitman**, p. 166, **SR** rules.

Dwarf: Use **Dwarven Technician**, p. 166, **SR** rules.

Troll: Use **Street Samurai**, p. 46, **SR** rules, with Troll modifiers and Mild Sunlight Allergy.

Security Officers: Use **Corp Security Guard**, p. 165, **SR** rules.

Info/Contacts

If subdued, any of the three hitmen will be willing to bargain with the information they have. They are, after all, mercenaries. Any of them knows quite a bit about international merc affairs.

A girl in her late teens approaches a runner. She is good-looking and seems naive about the realities of street life.

Quotes

"Uh…Hello. My name is Michelle. Michelle Gilroy."

"I was wondering…Well, that is, I need help, and Eve said you might be able to help me."

"You see, I'm afraid they're going to die out there."

Notes

Lauren Van Cleve is an efficient corporate spy, working for Natural Vat. A superior recently "asked" her to make a "deniable" run against one of the corp's rivals. Being naturally canny and wanting to preserve her own rear, Van Cleve decided to hire outsiders.

Deciding that she lacks time for the Mata Hari approach, she tries the "helpless little girl" ploy. If that fails, she can always fall back on the old "Please, sir, I'll do anything".

Her story is that her father and brother were analyzing nutrisoy compounds for flavor studies when they discovered a super-secret additive in "Aunt Sara's All Natural Nutrisoy Down-Home Brownie Mix". Later that day, the two were kidnapped. She learned about the super-secret compound from a "friend" who is a dataslave at Dixieland Edibles, manufacturer of the product. "Michelle" begs the runners to find the compound and her family members.

Archetypes

Michelle/Lauren: Use **Corporate Secretary**, p. 165, **SR** rules. Add Etiquette (Street) 4 and Firearms 5.

Info/Contacts

Lauren's budget for this is about 200,000 nuyen, but she plans to keep as much as possible for herself. Girl's gotta make a living.

An official from Eagle Security has asked the runners for an appointment this afternoon to discuss an old friend. When the man arrives, he asks a lot of questions.

Quotes

"You have known this 'Warlock', aka William Travis, for some five years now, is that correct?"

"In that time, have you ever known him to break the law or willfully harm corporate property?"

"Do you know any other of his friends who might tell me something about him?"

Notes

"Warlock" is a decker named Travis who has lost more decks than Radio Shack ever built, and so usually uses a terminal. He applied for a job at Eagle as a corp decker, and they're investigating whether he's a good security risk.

Most runners would see this as a sellout, but Travis is hiding, trying to to stay alive with a Yak "virus packet" he picked up on a million-to-one shot. He can't even unscramble the packet.

He picked up the thing by mistake, and now can't figure out how to get rid of it. Meanwhile, Yaks are looking everywhere for Warlock.

If the runners rail at Travis for becoming a "dataslave" for Eagle, Travis at first reacts with confusion, then with horror, and then takes off. This starts a beautiful four-way, with the runners wanting to learn what Travis has and who wants to kill him, the Yaks seeking to "neutralize" him and anyone he touches, and Travis ripping off money and hiring muscle with it, hoping desperately to escape. Finally, the corp cops are also looking for him because he's robbing banks to get money. Travis hangs out in the local "civic center", run by Madame Sheila.

Archetypes

Travis: Use Decker, p. 34, **SR**. Radio Shack PCD-100.

Madame Sheila: Use **Fixer**, p.167, **SR** rules. Charisma 6.

Info/Contacts

Madame Sheila's girls roam everywhere and see everything, so it is logical to question them. If the runners can persuade the girls that they mean no harm to Travis, maybe the girls will help (for a price).

The runners have received a small gift, curiously suited to their hobbies, along with a request to meet the "donor" early the next evening at a local bar. The donor turns out to be an attractive woman whose hair and clothing are of a paramilitary cut.

Quotes

"Good evening. Could we talk?"

"I'm here because your rep is one of the best."

"I need help, real bad."

Notes

Recently, the children of an Ares Macrotech vice president were kidnapped. During the crisis, Ares' security forces were hampered by the fact that the "perp" was an Ares executive.

Karen King, local director for Ares, wants no repeats. She has organized a Rapid Response Team, responsible only to her. This team will carry out special missions using only those members whose skills are needed. Kelly wants the runners' help voluntarily, and offers them gifts as a gesture of goodwill.

This encounter provides a convenient lead-in for future corporate-based adventures, as well as earning the runners a valuable ally.

Archetypes

Karen King: Use **Bounty Hunter**, p. 163, **SR** rules. Remove cyberarm.

Info/Contacts

Karen King is a tactical and political expert. In her work for Ares, she is honest and protective of their interests, a deadly combination for anyone who crosses her. In addition to her Ares Macrotech contacts, she has contacts among elite mercenary forces.

The runners have been dressed in monkey suits all evening, playing waiter until they get the high sign from the greeting-card writer they're supposed to exit. Unfortunately, Eagle Security moves first.

Quotes

"Hoi, punks. Bet you're real surprised to see us."

"Ain't that right, punk?"

"Looks like you kidnappers picked the wrong guy."

Notes

The runners are supposed to help Kasahiro Mataguchi, a jingle writer for Fuchifax, the greetings datafax firm, defect to another greeting fax firm named Cheerful Blossoms. In reality, Mataguchi intends to join Happy Memories, but wanted to create a diversion. He told Eagle that a contact had warned him about a kidnapping to take place at an office party. While Eagle is busy busting the runners and worrying about their implanted cortex bombs, he and Happy Memories' runners are waltzing out, clean as you please.

The Eagle Security officers will not believe that Mataguchi set up a defection, especially to Cheerful Blossoms, which is on the way out anyway. They also aren't going to believe that the runners are innocent, especially with the hardware they're sure to be packing. When the truth finally comes out, the runners will probably have used up some pretty hefty favors.

Archetypes

Eagle Security: Use **Street Cop**, p. 171, **SR** rules.

Mataguchi: Use **Corporate Secretary**, p. 165, **SR** rules. Add Special Skill of Writing Jingles 8.

Info/Contacts

About the only good thing to come of all this is that the runners should be able to get a jingle of their own at a reduced rate—if they ever have the dire need for one.

The characters are heading for their favorite bar, with no thoughts of wrongdoing in their greedy little minds. Suddenly, an Eagle Security car screeches to a halt almost at their feet. If not for wired reflexes, they'd be paste.

Quotes

"Hoi, chummers! What're a bunch like you doing out on a night like this?"

"Stop slottin' me. You don't smell of slush. You *reek* of it."

"Well, just to make sure, I think I'll follow you for a couple of hours."

Notes

This Sprawl cop is bored, and decided to have some fun with the characters when he spotted them. He won't take any physical action unless the characters do, but will be as insulting as possible until tired of the game. If the runners decide to walk away, he'll follow for five to ten minutes in the car, trying to provoke someone into saying something stupid. If the team plays it cool, he'll roar off eventually.

Archetypes

Eagle Cop: Use **Street Cop**, p. 171, **SR** rules. Chrysler-Nissan Patrol-1.

Info/Contacts

If the runners think of it, they may be able to direct this guy at an enemy. They might also somehow glean information about Eagle procedures from him.

The runners are hanging out at a bar, waiting for a contact to show up. On the other side of the room, four figures in a corner booth are talking and laughing loudly. Suddenly, one of them rises and walks across the room to where some Royal Reapers are sitting in a booth next to the runners'. As she comes into the light, it's obvious that's she's not only a knockout, but a cop.

Quotes

"You little jerks think you're so tough. Well, come on. Take a shot."

"Whassa' matter, big guy? You Rabid Rabbits can't handle one girl?"

"Oh, sorry about that. No, not his face. The mirror."

Notes

A bunch of rookie cops are out for their first night on the town since leaving the Academy. Eventually one of them boasts that no skirt cop is a match for a "real" one. The one skirt present thought that insulting enough to merit a response. Now she's jandering around the bar, determined to find some group (of guys, not girls) to insult and beat up to prove that she's tough.

If the Reapers don't give her satisfaction, she'll keep going until she finds someone who does.

If the runners try to get up to leave, they will immediately draw her attention and her sarcasm. If they sit tight, one of the Reapers will make a move and get pulverized, starting a general brawl, which should provide a much better chance to escape.

Archetypes

Female Rookie: Use **Street Cop**, p. 171, **SR** rules.
Male Rookies: Use **Corp Security Guard**, p. 165, **SR**.
Reapers: Use **Gang Member**, p. 39, **SR** rules.
King Reaper: Use **Gang Boss**, p. 167, **SR** rules.

Info/Contacts

The Reapers are the gang in control of the local turf. If the runners are already on good terms with them, helping the Reapers in this fight may be enough to get honorary gang membership. If the runners aren't on good terms, helping out now should change all that.

A runner is going about some routine business, when a young, well-built, well-armed male appears. He stands quietly in the background until the runner's current business is finished, much like a bodyguard. Then, he approaches.

Quotes

"You're a big name in town. Big names usually have big worries."

"You're big. You'll be bigger. I want to get in on the ground floor."

"A little guns, a little explosives…My mother always believed in a traditional education."

Notes

The ultimate professional, a young but ambitious cop has gone undercover to learn about the movers and shakers in the town, and perhaps to learn what lowtown is really like. The quickest way to do that is hiring out as a bodyguard. With his police/military training and the courage that only comes from inexperience, he thought that would be no problem.

Shylock Franklin soon learned that most lowtowners would not hire as a bodyguard someone they did not know. That's why he's approached this new band of runners.

Depending on how the group of runners acts, he may decide that they are more "just" than most cops. He may even decide to become a real runner.

Archetypes

Undercover Cop: Use **Former Company Man**, p. 37, **SR** rules.

Info/Contacts

None of the characters should realize that Shylock is an undercover cop. He has several cop contacts that he can use if things get tough. He also knows some access codes into the plex's SANs.

Eight A.M. A loud knock on the door. A runner stumbles over to it, holding his head and muttering. When he opens the door, his curses stop quickly at the sight of a man showing his shiny silver badge.

Quotes

"Callahan. Vice. Mind if I come in?"

"You ever see someone dive in front of a robotruck? Looks horrible. Blood everywhere."

"Real life ain't good enough after BTL. They do anything for that high. Anything. Even kill themselves."

Notes

Mack Johnson is a 20-year veteran. He's slept in garbage on stakeouts, brown-nosed little skanks who couldn't wipe their tail without him because they were someone's "pets," and held the line against the slime who want to run this city.

In the last seven months, a new BTL supplier has surfaced. Someone's bypassing "the Sicilian brotherhood" and the "honorable businessmen" and taking it directly to the street gangs. The chips are everywhere, as is the slogan, "One push and you're in Hightown forever."

It's got to stop. The cops can't touch the "local boys," but if someone doesn't, the entire city's in danger. Just as the runner is about to throw this guy out, the man says he's willing to forget that blowout last month at Ares. The one where the character got a little mixed up and emptied his HK into the R&D databanks?

Archetypes

Mack Johnson: Use **Plain clothes Cop**, p. 116, this book.

Info/Contacts

Mack's a good cop, just a little tired of all the politics. He wants to nail these BTL pushers, but the cops can't do it. He'll use anything he has to to get them.

It's seven-thirty in the morning after a hard night of partying, and this fraggin' cop won't stop asking his fraggin' questions!

Quotes

"Now let's go over this again…"

"You were where? Exactly, please."

"I'm sorry. I don't understand. Let's take it from the top. You were minding your own business when—?"

Notes

Meet Wilfred Jerome Royce. He's a new detective, recently come on board to replace a retired veteran.

He's supposed to investigate a little gang war. It seems that some street gangs have actually gotten together to sell the illegal BTL simsense chips, but the Yaks aren't willing to step aside.

Archetypes

Wilfred Jerome Royce: Use **Detective**, p. 35, **SR** rules. Subtract 2 from all stats (minimum 1).

Info/Contacts

Royce is new to the job, and doesn't really know what he's doing. He could be a source on anything from police procedures to police politicking.

The decker's in the Matrix, trying to sneak into the Police Department mainframe. Suddenly, a tall policeman on a horse trots up alongside him. The policeman has a gun sheathed, a blunderbuss of herculean proportions.

Quotes

"Morning. I'd like to talk to you."

"We've got a problem. You *and* me."

"How'd you like it if your deck started throwing off sparks. Into your EEG."

Notes

There's a virus loose in the system, though no one knows who put it there. It doesn't affect mainframes, but it shorts cyberdecks and terminals. With decks, it usually happens when someone's in the Matrix. The police have lost three deckers that way.

Rough Rider, the mounted policeman, is in charge of a cooperative effort to stop the virus before it gets worse. Deckers from all over are being asked to help. He wants to know if the player decker has any info on the virus, and if he will lend a hand to fight it.

Archetypes

Rough Rider: Use **Decker**, p. 35, **SR** rules. Add a Fuchi-5 with Level 1 Response Increase. Persona Programs rated 5.

Normal Decker: Use **Decker**. Subtract −1 from all skills (minimum 1).

Info/Contacts

Rider is out to stop the virus, and doesn't care how. If he has to break laws or reveal privileged information, so be it.

A tall, wiry man garbed in dark-green clothing approaches the runners one evening.

Quotes

"I have been told you may be able to assist me...I wish to stop the killing."

"My wild brothers have committed no crime. I must stop the wanton killing."

"The Great One has guided me to you. If you do not help me, I will die as they do."

Notes

Aaron Sly One is a loner from the nearby tribal lands. A group of city-based poachers have recently been preying on the local wolf population, killing them for their pelts. Though Sly One is not used to city ways, he has tracked the poachers to a nearby rooming house, and intends to confront them. He has been told that the player characters might help.

The six poachers, all low-class ruffians, can be suitably intimidated to stop their trapping. If too provoked, however, they will fight. They have assembled in a small apartment to split the last week's earnings.

Archetypes

Aaron Sly One: Use **Shaman**, p. 44, **SR** rules. He is a Wolf Shaman.

Poacher: Use **Squatter**, p. 170, **SR** rules. Arm half of them with Uzi IIIs and the other half with a sporting rifle of the gamemaster's choice.

Info/Contacts

Sly One could be a valuable source of information for activities outside the urban area, especially if a guide were needed.

Walking home one night, the player characters are strafed by a pair of Fire Elementals, who are apparently out for a night of fun on the town.

Quotes

"Oh man! I hate it when this happens!"

"I don't care where you find one! Just get me a fire extinguisher!"

"Not the clothes! Not the clothes!"

Notes

This is a definite case of being in the wrong place at the wrong time. The Elementals have just broken free of a fledgling magician. In escaping, they have, inexplicably, remained physical instead of fleeing into Astral Space.

The magician comes running after the Elementals, looking as though he's been through an inferno. He could use help from the characters to get the beings under control, or at least to neutralize them.

Archetypes

Elementals: Use **Fire Elemental**, p. 182, **SR**, Rating 4.

Magician: Use **Wiz-Kid Mage**, p. 121, this book.

Info/Contacts

While the Magician is not impressive, he does have an uncle, a first-class Hermetic Mage, who may just be looking for some bodyguards.

A shapely brunette with short, close-cropped hair, this sorceress certainly doesn't fit the typical mold. She is nevertheless a formidable mage involved in a contest with a rival mage. She needs your help.

Quotes

"The man's a pig. You have no idea what he's going to make me do if I lose."

"Ritual magic. That's what I said. There's a nasty Sending coming down on me right now."

"Please help me, or it's the end for me."

Notes

Carol Tyrell is a veteran sorceress whose misfortune is being too boastful. After carrying her boasts too far the other evening, she found herself in a Contest of Power. The battle was supposed to remain magical, but the terms did not prevent either participant from using non-magical power. Tyrell blew her Ritual Casting early on, and is now waiting for her opponent's hammer to fall. She knows where he is, and wants to disrupt his Sending.

Her opponent is an Ork Shaman who lives in a warehouse with a dozen other Ork followers. Tyrell wants the Sending disrupted, but none of the Orks hurt. She can afford to pay.

Archetypes

Carol Tyrell: Use **Street Mage**, p. 45, **SR** rules. Add 10 Force Points to appropriate Spells.

Ork Shaman: Use **Ork Shaman**, p. 115, this book.

Ork Followers: Use **Pedestrian (Ork)**, p. 116, this book.

Info/Contacts

Help Tyrell get her butt out of hot water, and she will be grateful enough to offer magical backup on a future run, or else will provide some magical contacts.

This Sasquatch is tawny-colored, with big, saucer-like eyes and an affecting grin. When first seen, he is wounded and fending off the local go-gang, who have been pelting him with rocks and the occasional bullet.

Quotes

"(Wolf-howling noises) Get away! Run away!"

"(Machine gun noises) You dirty rats!!"

"(Howls of pain)."

Notes

The Sasquatch is only able to communicate in the special Perkins-Athapascan sign language designed especially for communication with his kind. Odds are no one around can speak the language, so the characters will have to use gestures, mime, and sound effects (which the Sasquatch so love).

He's lost, far from home, and wounded. Worse, the local street gangs have decided to make a game out of getting his scalp. All he wants is to heal up and go home. Left alone, he will surely die.

Archetypes

Sasquatch: Use **Sasquatch Entertainer**, p. 117, this book.

Go-Gang Members: Use **Gang Member**, p. 39, **SR** rules. All have Suzuki Aurora racing bikes.

Info/Contacts

This Sasquatch is an influential member of his community, located within the tribal lands. If the runners become involved in an adventure outside the Sprawl, he would be an invaluable contact.

He's dressed straight out of some Shakespearean play, and looks almost old enough to have known the Bard. Yet there is an edge of great power about him.

Quotes

"Pardon me, I understand one of you is a practitioner of the Great Arts. Is that so?"

"Magic is indeed an Art, like sculpting or newscasting."

"The time has come to pass everything I know on to another. Why you, among so many others? Your eyes are the right color."

Notes

Porter Alwyn is a veteran of the Hermetic Arts, highly respected as a trail-blazer. Now time has begun to take its toll and he feels his power slipping. If he can pass on his knowledge, it would be a joy to him. He's never had a family, never even taken an apprentice.

His small apartment is filled with mementos of his career. It may even contain clues to a decades-old magical mystery.

Buried deep in one closet is a deed showing his ownership of a building in one of the districts of the Sprawl. Who knows what's there now.

Archetypes

Porter Alwyn: Use **Former Wage Mage**, p. 38, **SR** rules. Reduce Body, Strength, and Quickness by 1. Reduce Magic by 2, but add 2 to each Magic-related skill. Add 2 points to all listed Spells. He also has a Rating 4 Basic Power Focus, with enough force for all the Spells.

Info/Contacts

Alwyn is a fount of information about magic, history, and important people. His insights into the why and wherefore of the world is worth the price of admission.

She is tall and thin, with gold-streaked platinum hair that matches her expressive eyes. Her clothes are loose and ill-matched, and her face has a strange, haunted look to it.

Quotes

"Someone has taken the eggs. They are very…rare…and we must return them to the wild."

"Please, you must help me. The eggs' mother is desperate to find them."

"They are the eggs of a rare golden eagle. Without their mother, the eggs will not mature, and without her children…I'm not sure what the mother would do."

Notes

The woman is actually an eagle shapeshifter from the tribal lands beyond the city. Several days ago, a local conservationist "rescued" her eggs from the wild and has taken them to "safety." The shapeshifter is heartbroken. Having tracked her brood to the city, she now needs assistance from the players.

Nigel Jones, head of the local Wilderness Conservation Group, did not realize the eggs belonged to an eagle shapeshifter. He took them to help prevent extinction of the golden eagle. When located, Jones insists that the eggs be hatched and raised in captivity.

How will the characters get the eggs? When Jones sees the disguised shapeshifter, he claims that the woman is a magical animal who also belongs in the care of a zoo. He offers a great deal of money.

Archetypes

Eagle Shapeshifter: Use **Eagle Shapeshifter**, p. 187, **SR** rules.

Nigel Jones: Use **Metahuman Rights Activist**, p. 167, **SR** rules. Ecology 3.

Info/Contacts

The eagle shapeshifter is unaccustomed to "civilized" life, which is what will give her away even though she is trying desperately to conceal her true nature.

Some Orks who the player characters know come running up to them late one evening. Seems they were knocking around the sewers when they encountered a hidden chamber, complete with resident vampire. Guess who's next on his blood donation list?

Quotes

"Teeth bigger than mine! I swear!"

"You'll help us? Right? Just like last time?"

"Well..um...he was right behind us..."

Notes

Nicholas Jordan is happy being a vampire, for he loves the power and control. He plays to the hilt the part of the distinguished, cultured vampire. The sewer chamber is his primary back-up pad, and he wants to protect its secret. Though he generally dislikes Ork blood, he will have to make the group who found him his evening meal. And anyone else they may have told will become a fine dessert.

Archetypes

Vampire: Use **Vampire**, p. 188, **SR** rules.

Orks: Use **Pedestrian (Ork)**, p. 116, this book.

Info/Contacts

If negotiation is used instead of violence, the runners might persuade Jordan to hire the Orks as guardians for his crypt.

Up ahead, the characters see a pretty young woman making a call inside a vidphone booth. Outside, a group of ghouls are rattling the door. Ghouls needing to make a phone call? Or have they other, more interesting things in mind?

Quotes

"Hey, lady, you gonna be long? Heh-heh."

"What's it to you, chummer?"

"I'm sorry. All lines to Lone Star Security are busy right now. The first available operator will…"

Notes

These three ghouls are a gang of sorts who have decided not to hide in the shadows any longer (ghouls are people, too, ya know). On their first night out, they've decided to do some terrorizing. The woman in the vidphone booth seemed a prime choice, until the characters came along…

Once the player characters take action against the ghouls, the woman makes her own move. Turns out she wasn't a helpless victim, just smart enough to know she was outnumbered. She's a street samurai, a bona fide razorgirl more than willing to prove it.

Archetypes

Millie: Use **Street Samurai**, p. 46, **SR** rules.

Ghouls: Use **Ghoul**, p. 183, **SR** rules.

Info/Contacts

Millie is new in town. In gratitude for the runners' help, she might connect the runners with other samurai contacts in the city, once she finds them.

While walking down the street, the runners laugh to see a parked van rocking steadily. Just as they are about to harass the van's amorous occupants, the back door opens and a half-devoured body falls out. Before the characters can react, a gold and red animal form springs out and bounds away.

Quotes

"Holy &*$#^#%@$!"

"It's a griffin! I think its a griffin!"

"Get it offa me!"

Notes

A griffin has wandered into town and gone on a killing frenzy, which is abnormal behavior for this creature. It has been driven mad by a wound wracking its body with pain and poison. Inflicted by a hunter's poisoned arrow a week ago, the wound is large, suppurating, and very visible on the griffin's left flank.

If the characters have their wits enough about them to help heal the creature, the griffin will break off its attack and flee for home. The grateful critter might, alternatively, decide to adopt the group, following them everywhere.

Archetypes

Griffin: Use **Griffin**, p. 184, **SR** rules.

Info/Contacts

Having a griffin as a pet definitely violates the local ASPCA rules.

A casual acquaintance is in a panic. Following a fun evening on the town, he woke up this morning on a park bench, and immediately discovered all his Power Focuses and Spell Locks missing.

Quotes

"You don't understand! They lead right to me."

"I should save them the trouble and jump off a bridge."

"Do you know how long it took me to make those?"

Notes

The young Street Mage is in luck. The thieves who took his valuable magic items are a bunch of park squatters who were peeved to find him on a favorite bench. They've got the items all spread out in another area of the park, where they're sitting around trying to figure out how to make the magic work.

One of the player characters should realize that the astral connection between a magical item and its maker runs both ways. It should be a simple matter for their friend to pop into Astral Space to assense the threads. The only problem is his terror of Astral Space.

Even if the runners can persuade him to try, it will take time. By now, the squatters may have already begun to sell the items. Seems the mage who owns them has some enemies…

Archetypes

Street Mage: Use **Street Mage**, p. 45, **SR** rules.

Squatters: Use **Squatter**, p. 170, **SR** rules.

Info/Contacts

Help this guy retrieve his magical items and he will owe the runners a big one.

Things seem calm enough when suddenly the characters hear the deafening sound of motorcycles roaring through the night. As they turn, prepared to confront a go-gang, the first powerballs start going off. Guess again, chummers.

Quotes

"Hoi! Hoi! Look at 'um run!!"

"Blast em, Jimmy! Roast em!"

"WWAAAHHOOOO!!!"

Notes

While the bikes and the way these folks ride make them technically a go-gang, their magic makes them a wizzer gang. Wiz-kid mages, as the datafaxes call them. They combine the "traditional" go-gang's love of wild rampaging with out-of-control magical power.

Tonight, they're after people instead of just property. So what if these guys seem to be runners? That'll just make it more fun.

An additional complication: one of the wizzer gang members is the son of an important local exec, and the corp's security cops are out looking for the brat.

Archetypes

Wiz-Kid Mages: Use **Wiz-Kid Mage**, p. 121, this book.

Security Forces: Four **Corporate Security Guards**, p. 165, **SR** rules. One **Street Samurai**, p. 46, **SR** rules. One **Former Wage Mage**, p. 38, **SR** rules.

Info/Contacts

Help the executive nab his son, and he'll be grateful. On the other hand, he might not like it that somebody outside the corp knows something that could be used as blackmail.

With that rail-thin body, ashen pallor, and wild red-eyed stare, he could be a vampire. But he's throwing spells. Wait a minute? Spells! What's going on here?

Quotes

"Flesh of the earth, I need your soul this night."

"I must feed!"

"You will share with me your essence, samurai. And you will die."

Notes

Driven mad by the ebbs and flows of his power and by a radical burn from a BTL chip, this sorcerer now believes he is a vampire who must feed on the essence of others to survive. He's a lost soul, and no amount of reasoning will get through to him.

Even killing won't be the end of him. His psyche is so geared up that he will only reappear as a ghost to haunt the player characters. Hey, maybe he really is a vampire…

Archetypes

Mad Sorcerer: Use **Former Wage Mage**, p. 38, **SR**.

Info/Contacts

Unknown to the characters, there is a 50,000-nuyen bounty out on this guy.

A few months ago, a runner's armorer died when his house exploded with him in it. Needing some equipment real quick, the runner used a Dwarf armorer who wasn't yet well-known. Now the Dwarf has plenty of clients, and a soft spot for the runner who got him started. Indeed, he'd like to do him a favor.

Quotes

"I've been working on them for years, and I think I've finally perfected them."

"Should have better hitting power than anything on the market."

"The price? You're a friend."

Notes

Smith's a former company Dwarf who was working on prototypical "Slayer" ammo when he had to leave his former employ rather hurriedly. Now it looks as though he's found the formula and he wants his friend to be the first one to have the new ammo. All he's asking the runner to do is test the ammo.

The gamemaster decides exactly what this ammunition does. It could be useless, or nothing more than ordinary ammo. Or it could be better, even earth-shattering. If it's as good as Smith thinks, however, he will never allow anyone else to have the formula (whose previous version was stolen by the corp). It will take him a while to make each bullet (the first lot consists of only ten), and the work must be sandwiched between that of his clients. If the ammo is good, it might best be saved for emergencies.

Archetypes

Smith: Use **Dwarven Technician**, p. 166, **SR** rules. Change Computer Skills to Metallurgy and Gunsmithing.

Info/Contacts

Smith has corp contacts and could help the runners to contact other Dwarfs.

Tallock has stolen the Infernal Diamond to show he's more than a small-time thief. He's invited the runners to his place to prove how wrong they were about him.

Quotes

"Isn't it bee-you-tee-ful?"

"Have you ever seen such luster?"

"Puts the Hope Diamond to shame."

Notes

The Infernal Diamond is displayed on a large pedestal in the Dwarf's small flat. It symbolizes Tallock's triumph over everyone who ever laughed at him, and he would rather die than give up or sell the diamond.

This can lead to all sorts of interesting complications, as common thieves or even larcenous shadowrunners try to steal it. Musn't forget the Diamond's previous owner, either.

Tallock doesn't know he only has a paste duplicate of the Infernal Diamond, whose purpose was to protect the real gem from theft. Everyone believes it's the real thing, however, and the previous owner will play along with the game to continue to protect his treasure.

Archetypes

Tallock: Use **Gang Member**, p. 39, **SR**.

Previous Owner: Use **Mr. Johnson**, p. 170, **SR**.

Info/Contacts

Though not a great thief, Tallock is a good one. He can get into places where taller runners won't fit, or into others where they would look out of place. If they are careful not to deliberately wound Tallock's pride, he could be a valuable ally.

The Wrangler is a Dwarf fixer of great repute, known for using only Metahumans. So when he gives your group a call for a job, it's news.

Quotes

"Ordinarily, I don't use Humans, but…"

"Simple. Metahumans get the shaft from most fixers, and I even the score."

"I need something done that Metahumans can't do."

Notes

Fall Fest will take place in two weeks. It is the Metahumans' annual street fair to celebrate the harvest season and the "brotherhood of man." Humanis Policlub members always use force to keep other Humans away, however, resulting in a purely Metahuman affair.

Wrangler believes the Policlub is going to try something worse than usual this year. As the club members are all Humans, he feels that Humans would best serve to foil them. Fall Fest is an important happening in town, and so this mission should take on major dimensions.

Unknown to anyone is the real threat, an assassin hired to kill Wrangler on the last night of the festival. The assassin will strike with a sniper-scope-equipped rifle from the organizational trailer nearby.

Kerry Taylor, the noted human rights reporter, will be there with a camera crew. She will try to remain on the sidelines, but evidence of bigotry will anger her. She will not reveal her talent unless necessary.

Archetypes

Wrangler: Use **Fixer**, p. 167, **SR** rules, with Dwarf modifiers. Add Etiquette (Corporate) to match his Street.

Assassin: Use **Elven Hitman**, p. 166, **SR** rules. Note that he is Human.

Fair Attendee: Use **Bartender**, p. 163, **SR** rules.

Kerry Taylor: Use **Former Wage Mage** (Healer Orientation), p. 38, **SR** rules.

Info/Contacts

Wrangler knows how to get his hands on most fetishes and other items used in magic rituals. He also has the normal skills of any street fixer.

A contact lets you know about a simple little courier job. The guy who needs help is a pleasant Dwarf named Morgan, an inventor who's working on a project for Walker Data Systems.

Quotes

"It's a modular hyperphasic integrator."

"What does it *do*? Sound out the name!"

"It helps with data transmissions, and it's cheap."

Notes

Morgan has developed a new component for use in data transmission. What it does is boost the strength of computer data transmissions for easier access across poor communication lines. Though the device cannot be used for secure data, it could cut the cost of non-secure data transmission by as much as 9 percent.

Morgan has been working privately on this invention ever since he caused some unauthorized explosions on company property. That's why he needs someone else to take the integrator to the corporate R&D office. It shouldn't be too difficult, except for some "troubleshooters" a low-grade corp exec has sent to make sure he gets the integrator.

Archetypes

Morgan: Use **Dwarven Technician**, p. 166, **SR**.

Low-Grade corp: Use **City Official**, p. 164, **SR**.

Corp Agents: Use **Corporate Security Guard**, p. 165, **SR**.

Info/Contacts

Morgan is one of the original practitioners of weird science. If the runners need a technological device, expect him to come up with one that is quite bizarre. (The coal-powered air conditioner still raises eyebrows in some circles.)

Two nights ago, a firefight broke out between two shadowrunner teams, one Dwarven and one Human. The fight ended with most of the Dwarfs and all the Humans dead. Now one of the Dwarf survivors wants to talk with the player characters about a job.

Quotes

"Most Humans don't want to get involved when they hear about something like this. You that kind?"

"Funny. I thought you tall types outlawed slavery 200 years ago."

"Some fantasy freak wants to use Dwarf slaves in his mines."

Notes

Dalthurn and his friends have learned about a slavery ring specializing in selling Dwarfs to South American and African mining companies. His group geeked the runners the slavers

hired for protection, but the Dwarfs need help to carry off the big one.

The slavers have the freighter *Lady Stephanie* anchored at the docks. The slaves were loaded on board earlier tonight, and the ship will set sail as soon as an engine repair part arrives. Dalthurn wants to stop the *Stephanie* before it raises anchor. Ten guards will be in a dispatcher's hut next to the freighter until it sails.

Archetypes

Dalthurn: Use **Merc**, p. 40, **SR** rules. Apply Dwarf modifiers. No cyberware.

Slaver Guard: Use **Street Cop**, p. 171, **SR** rules.

Slaver Overseer: Use **Gang Boss**, p. 167, **SR** rules.

Freed Slave: Use **Pedestrian** (due to weakness), p. 116, this book.

Info/Contacts

Dalthurn is not an important Dwarf, but his tale of Humans who helped him rescue other Dwarves will be told time and again. The story will help the runners in future dealings with Dwarfs (and their allies).

Jay Penman, a Dwarf street samurai of the player characters' aquaintance needs some help.

Quotes

"Some friends of mine have got a propblem."

"As far as I'm concerned, the building is theirs. Lordy, they've been living there for five years."

"Yeah, so what if they're Elves? I'm not supposed to be friends with Elves?"

Notes

Jay's friends are Elven squatters, three families' worth, and they've been living in an abandoned building for over five years. A few days ago, the Genom Corporation informed the Elves that the building was being torn down and they would have to move. The families have nowhere else to go.

Jay claims that common law makes the Elf families owners of the building, but the corp's enforcers don't see it that way. In two days, they're going to start bulldozing, regardless of whether or not the families have moved out The Dwarf wants to stop Genom, fast.

Archetypes

Turpin: Use **Street Samurai,** p. 46, **SR**, but apply Dwarf racial modifiers.

Elven Squatters (14): Use **Squatter,** p. 170, **SR**.

Genom Enforcers (5): Use **Bodyguard,** p 97, this book..

Info/Contacts

Because Genom is publicity-shy right now, any threat of exposure will be effective at getting the negotiations to the point of finding a new place for the Elves to live.

There is an Elf with an attitude in town, and he's intent on rubbing it off on you. His garb looks straight out of some medieval fantasy. He claims to be a Paladin of the High Lord of Tir Tairngire.

Quotes

"Such a foul place is this city. A dark day, indeed, when I first I breathed its so-called 'air'."

"You stare? Have you never seen a Strident Paladin of the Fifth Mark? Your loss."

"Those snide comments are ill-advised, my friends. I am bearing a Martial Writ that allows me combat rights in all lands."

Notes

First, this guy is no "Strident Paladin of the Fifth Mark," because there is no such thing. He's never been to Tir Tairngire, and barely knows how to pronounce it. He's an Elf named Walter Blothum, who is caught up in a chip-induced fantasy. That doesn't make him any less dangerous. A former member of a local security firm, he's an able warrior.

He'll spin an involved story about a missing artifact and the Elven High Lord's desire to reclaim it. Then he'll lead any gullible player characters deep into the worst neighborhood, straight into a heap of gang trouble.

Archetypes

Ethayn Silvervane (Walter Blothum): Use **Elven Hitman**, p. 166, **SR** rules.

Info/Contacts

Apart from his Paladin fantasy, Blothum is a skilled warrior. Once he gets to know the characters, he might share with them his former employer's deep, dark secrets.

Wrapped in homespun cloth and carrying a hand-carved walking staff, this Elf is apparently confused by a map of the local transit lines. While he's theorizing about the meanings of the various colors and symbols, the runners notice members of a local thrill gang about to set him up for a fall.

Quotes

"'Transfer at the Park for all crosstown and downtown express lines, except during periods of peak usage, at which time…'"

"Excuse me, young one, could you please explain to me the term 'exact change only'?"

"Aren't all those pins in your face painful?"

Notes

Galen, an Elf Mage from the nearby Elven lands, has been sent by his master to "learn the ways of man". Thus far, he's learned the fine art of sloppy-soy slurping and ridden the monorail six times around the city. Now it's time to try the complex bus system, but he's so confused that he fails to notice the Crucifixers ready to pounce.

Archetypes

Galen: Use **Elf Mage**, p. 100, this book.

The Crucifixers: Use **Gang Member**, p. 39, **SR** rules. At least 1D6 + 2 gang members are present.

Info/Contacts

If Galen survives his stay in the city, the characters may persuade him to give them a tour of the small community where he lives. He may also be of help against the rabid Dwarf group that's been harassing them.

The runners have been warned by all their contacts to be very careful of this one. They're to meet with an Elf fixer named Chalen. The hints of gray in his hair show his age, which is odd for an Elf. You meet him in one of the usual places.

Quotes

"I understand you are very good, very reliable. That's good. I need both."

"Money is no problem. You do the job. I pay you the money. No problem."

"There are some Elves in this city that I want hurt. Perhaps you've heard of them, a group who call themselves the Ancients?"

Notes

Chalen represents a group of power-broker Elves who believe the Ancients biker gang may be on the verge of expanding into a policlub. To prevent that, they want to show the Ancients that someone doesn't approve. But, remember, the mission is to hurt the gang, not to massacre them.

The fixer can provide some information about the Ancients' activities, but the team will also have to do surveillance. They will only learn the Ancients' routine patterns, however.

At the gamemaster's option, a stunning Elven woman approaches the runners shortly before they are to make their move on the Ancients. The contact takes place in a busy public place. She walks up to one or more runners, tells them that hitting the Ancients would be bad for the characters' health, then smiles and walks away. If the characters try to follow, a sufficient number of Elven Street Samurai will delay them long enough for their mistress to get clear.

It is the gamemaster's choice as to what exactly is going on. It's obviously a power struggle between at least two Elven groups, but the issue is not clear.

Archetypes

Chalen: Use **Fixer**, p. 167, **SR** rules. Apply Elf racial modifiers.

The Woman: Use **Elf Mage**, p. 100, this book.

The Ancients: Use **Gang Member**, p. 39, **SR** rules. Apply Elven racial modifiers.

Info/Contacts

Either Chalen, the woman, or the Ancients could provide an inroad into the intricacies of Elven politics.

Tall and gaunt, the Elf has the look of a wild thing. Yet people listen to him, whether man, woman, Elf, or Ork. Alamos 20,000 has also recently gotten wind of him.

Quotes

"The cities will fall by man's own hand and again we shall return to the womb of nature."

"The conspiracy of the Humans and the Dragons will destroy the world."

"The Day of Darkness is at hand! We must purge the land of corruption and darklight..."

Notes

David has seen a vision of a future that includes only Elves and their allies. His dozen or so street-corner sermons in the Sprawl have drawn huge, multi-racial crowds over the past two weeks. Eagle Security has been unwilling to interfere, perhaps verifying reports of Eagle execs often present at the Elf's sermons.

The local chapter of Alamos 20,000 has vowed publicly to lynch the Elf. The player characters know that David will be preaching in a nearby park tomorrow, and that an Alamos 20,000 supporter will attempt to kill him.

Does David really have visions, and are they accurate? Is he the Elven successor to Howling Coyote, whom the Elves of the ghetto have been awaiting?

Archetypes

David: Use the **Elf Mage**, p. 100, this book. Delete all magic and magical skills. Add Leadership 8 and Negotiation 9.

Alamos Assassin: Use **Street Mage**, p. 45, **SR**.

Info/Contacts

People of all races flock to hear David speak, and his presence inspires strong feelings of brotherhood in the crowd. The player characters could meet just about anybody here.

He's not what you expected. When your fixer said an Elf hunter needed help tracking a wild animal in the city, you figured the guy would be somebody straight out of Tolkien. (By the way, that is a Walther WA2100 sniper rifle she's carrying.)

Quotes

"He's dangerous. No telling what he might do."

"I've been tracking him across half the damn country and most of the tribal lands. He's pretty wily."

"No, not an animal. I never said that. He's a Banshee."

Notes

Sylvia Knorr has been a hunter almost all her life. She was born to Human parents, but was raised in the tribal lands. In the past year, she has been hunting Lucas, but he remains always a step ahead of her. Having learned that he's in the Sprawl, she decided to get some local help in finding him.

Lucas will seek out an abandoned building in the poorest neighborhood, preying on the local vagrants and squatters. According to Knorr, Lucas lives only to kill. Though some claim that Banshees are sentient, and may even be infected with a HMHVV, she will argue that he is an animal.

The eventual confrontation with Lucas will prove little either way. His actions might be attributed to a purely animal intelligence, but they could easily be those of a sentient who has lost his grip on reality.

Archetypes

Sylvia Knorr: Use **Bounty Hunter**, p. 163, **SR** rules. Apply Elven racial modifiers.

Lucas: Use **Banshee**, p. 179, **SR** rules.

Info/Contacts

Sentient or not, Lucas behaves like a crazed animal. When the player characters eventually confront him, he will be living among the remains and bones of many bodies, most of them children's.

Shorter than average, John Fallow is an average-looking Elf. His hair is pulled back severely from his face, accenting the anger in his expression. John Fallow is out for blood.

Quotes

"I will not let him get away with this, even if it kills us both."

"She was everything to me. I see her face on everyone in the crowd, or hear her voice in the wind singing through the trees at night."

"The only clues are the name 'Oliver' and a drink coupon from the Corporate Bums and Indigents Club."

Notes

Three nights ago, Fallow's Human girlfriend was slain by a man at a local night spot. He knew of her involvement with an Elf and was giving her a hard time. At the night spot, he offered the CBI coupon in exchange for a drink ("we honor all competitors' coupons") and used the name Oliver. Two hours later, she was dead and a man matching Oliver's description was seen fleeing the scene.

The gamemaster should make it difficult to follow Oliver, creating a twisting path of hints, clues, false sightings, and other obstacles to keep the search exciting. Who is Oliver? Why did he kill the girl? Was it true that he loved her? Was it a case of mistaken identity? And what if Oliver were using a mask spell?

Archetypes

John Fallow: Use **Elf Mage**, p. 100, this book.

Info/Contacts

An interesting variation on this plot might be that the stress of magic has made Fallow mentally unstable, and that it was he who killed the girl under the paranoid delusion that she was seeing someone named Oliver. Of course, to do the actual killing, he became Oliver.

1

Someone the runners know, perhaps even one of the player characters, has fallen behind in his loan-shark payments. The collector, Bobby Black Bottom, is usually easy to placate. Unfortunately, the new boy in town is a Troll, and even bigger than usual.

Quotes

"Bobby? I'm his son. You can call me Adopted."

"I'm also his 'business partner'."

"Da book says you owe 14 hundred in loans and over 15 grand in penalties and DocWagon bills. Markers or certified stix only, chummer."

Notes

From now on, Adopted takes all the hard-line collection cases. He will talk to the runners (or their friend) once. He will accept being put off once, and once only. If someone tries to get smart, then Adopted will calmly and efficiently remove a leg. Nothin' personal, chummer. Strictly business.

Adopted is surprisingly intelligent. Whenever outclassed, he will retreat and call in back-up. As long as he is treated with respect and the debtor shows a willingness to pay, he will even agree to work out new terms of payment. (With a Troll loan collector, who wouldn't be "willing to pay"?)

Adopted is perfectly fair. If he damages someone's leg/arm/other vital organ, he will deduct 50 percent of the hospital expenses from the debt.

Archetypes

Adopted (real name Josh): Use **Troll Bouncer**, p. 173, **SR** rules. Intelligence 4, Firearms 5, and some body armor. Mild Silver Allergy.

Bobby: Use **Squatter**, p. 170, **SR** rules. Change Special Skills to Firearms and Negotiation.

Back-up: Six **Troll Bouncers** with body armor.

Info/Contacts

Adopted knows both Metahumans and other loan sharks and collectors.

2

In what has to be the granddaddy of bad timing, the runners come upon a group of large people in an alley at night. As they open fire, the flashes reveal their opponents to be Trolls.

Quotes

"Get da breederz!"

"Don't kill them. Their murdering ain't for us."

"We are Trolls! We alone honor the land, and destroy those who would harm it."

Notes

Several weeks ago, an up-and-coming exec named Roger Harris saved his corp 25,000 nuyen per month by contracting with a new waste disposal company. He got a 25,000-nuyen bonus on his stick, and forgot about it. The dumping company wasn't so lucky, though.

When the government refused their application to dump wastes, they had to find a place to dump the stuff before it melted through their trucks. Because it was dark and the place was not well-marked, they dropped the load in a local Troll burial ground.

Thanks to Troll thermographic eyes, someone saw the trucks, and a group of Trolls tried to block their way. Most of the drivers were able to drive around the Trolls standing in the road, but one bright sarariman decided to floor it and drive right through. He wasted a Troll, but that stunt also wasted his engine.

The Trolls learned the dump company's name from papers inside the cab. Then they paid the company a visit to find out the name of the driver who killed their friend.

Finding Roger's name among the files in the dumpers' office, the Trolls mistakenly pinned the blame on him. They also believe the player characters are his bodyguard. If Roger can't escape, his only hope is to persuade the Trolls of his innocence. Lotsa luck, Rog.

Archetypes

Roger: Use **City Official**, p. 164, **SR** rules.

Troll Leader: Use **Bear Shaman**, p. 75, **SR** rules, with Troll modifiers.

Other Trolls 1–4: Use **Troll Bouncer**, p. 173, **SR**.

Info/Contacts

Roger is a junior exec with connections to many young corporators. The Trolls have connections to most Amerind communities.

3

Five Trolls are gathered around an old van. These guys look like pirates from an old movie, all wearing eye patches and one even has a peg leg! The van is painted like a pirate ship. The Trolls call out insults and snide comments to everyone who passes.

Quotes

"Avast, ye breeders! Heave it 'r we'll blow ya off da street!"

"What've we here? A group of wealthy merchants, eh? At 'em, lads!"

"No little breeder escapes Cap'n Crook!"

Notes

These Trolls are simsense chip abusers, particularly those set in the buccaneer era. When they're not off in their own world, they try to act like their heroes.

These Trolls are out for "booty," and don't care where it comes from. They decide that the runners are British officers, men of means who deserve to be "avasted" by privateers. They will start out by wrestling the "bloody lobsterbacks." If the runners pull out their weapons, the Trolls will draw swords and use them.

Archetypes

Trolls: Use **Troll Bouncer**, p. 173, **SR** rules. Raise Armed Combat to 4.

Info/Contacts

Though a bit strange, these fellows have their hearts in the right place. They could easily be convinced to help a "damsel in distress" or to attack a "British fort."

A friend of the runners has a problem. He had a wonderful time out on the town with a lady last night, until some guy showed up, demanding a huge chunk of money. The runners' chum got annoyed and slugged the guy, then took a beating from the other guy's Troll bodyguard.

Quotes

"Da guy hit da boss. Da boss is in da hospital."

"I dunno. Da boss ain't in no condition to talk. If he could, he'd be sayin' how angry he is."

"Lessee. Da boss's hospital bill…Ten thousand for da hospital, four hundred for, uh, services rendered."

Notes

Eric, the runner's friend, spent the evening with Sheila, a girl from an expensive escort service. He didn't realize that was the deal until her "manager" showed up with his bodyguard to settle accounts. Eric slugged the manager, then got clobbered by the bodyguard.

After the docs worked on Eric, the bodyguard took him to an undisclosed location. The characters can get Eric back by paying the 400 nuyen for his evening with Sheila plus twice the current hospital bill for her manager. That guy has been in at 500 nuyen a day ever since the scuffle with Eric.

Archetypes

Eric: Use **Talismonger**, p. 172, **SR** rules.

Sheila: Use **Corporate Secretary,** p. 165, **SR** rules.

Manager: Use **City Official**, p. 164, **SR** rules.

Bodyguard: Use **Troll Bouncer**, p. 173, **SR** rules.

Info/Contacts

Al, the manager, knows most legal and illegal escort service owners in the city, while Sheila knows most of the escorts. Darik, the bodyguard, knows most others in his line of work.

As the runners enter a bar, they hear loud, raucous singing. About 80 people are present, celebrating some occasion. Among them are a number of Trolls. Almost everyone in the bar, including the Trolls, seems more than a little drunk.

Quotes

"ANNNNNND WEEEEEE ALLLLLL GOOOO DOOOOWWWWWNNNN TOGETHER!" (sung)

"Howdy, breeder!"

"We-—We— We— I forgot what I was gonna say. Oh yeah. Your mother played with Elves!"

Notes

The runners have come to the bar to meet a contact, who appears to be late. What happened was that the contact took off when he saw all the Trolls. While the characters sit down to wait, everyone in the bar gets even more drunk.

Sooner or later, someone is going to make a comment that a Troll will take the wrong way, setting off a bar brawl. Imagine the wildest bar fight scenes from old Westerns, only with Trolls involved.

Archetypes

Trolls: Use **Street Cop**, p. 171, **SR** rules. (If they weren't drunk, it would be **Troll Bouncer** or **Ork Mercenary**.)

Humans: Use **Squatter**, p. 170, **SR** rules. (If they weren't drunk, it would be **Bartender** or **Street Cop**.)

Info/Contacts

After the fight, the runners may be trying to figure out where their contact went. One of the Trolls may say, "Short guy? 'Bout this high? Brown hair? Yeah, he came in, turned white, 'n went out 'bout an hour before da fight. Sumthin' musta scared 'im."

One of the runners is riding home on his Rapier late one night, when he hears a woman shriek in pain and fear. Reaching the alley from which the scream came, he finds a woman's body in a pool of blood. Just then, the cops show up.

Quotes

"You watch him, Link. I'll call for back-up!"

"The hell with that. *You* watch him and *I'll* call for back-up!"

"Hold it right there, chummer! (aside) We finally got the Carlin Avenue killer!"

Notes

The Carlin Avenue Killer has been murdering people and driving the cops nuts. He strikes in the dead of night, always kills women (usually alone), and always uses a knife. The cops have been trying, unsuccessfully, to catch him for weeks. Now, at last, they've got him red-handed, standing over his latest victim.

Even after the cops realize their mistake and let the runner go, they'll maintain a watch on him until the real Carlin Avenue Killer is caught. For the average runner (who goes around breaking at least one law every minute), that could be a disaster. The fastest way to get the cops off his back will be to find the Killer.

Ever wonder what would happen if a Troll got his hands on "Jack the Ripper" BTL chips? Well, that's the Carlin Avenue Killer: an insane Troll wandering at night (allergic to sunlight), thinking he's Jack the Ripper.

Archetypes

Cops: Use **Street Cop**, p. 171, **SR** rules.

Killer: Use **Ork Mercenary**, p. 41, **SR** rules.

Info/Contacts

The cops aren't going to be happy about runners interfering in their business, but they're even less happy about a killer on the loose. If the runners are clever, however, they may end up making friends with a couple of cops who could one day provide info or back-up.

A group of Orks approaches, smirking and chuckling. There are slightly more of them than the runners, and they all are armed.

Quotes

"Hoi, wimps! What'cha got fer us?"

"Gi'it up, chummer. Ya think that toy gun's gonna hurt Orks? No way."

"Never ask fer who da bell rings, 'er someone'll clobber ya wit'it!"

Notes

This gang of Orks is out for a good time, which they define differently than do Humans. For this band, it means relieving any Humans, Elves, or Dwarfs they meet of any money they're carrying. (Forget Trolls. These Orks ain't stupid.)

If the runners are not in great fighting shape at the moment, they can buy the Orks off at about 100 nuyen each. The Orks are numerous, but not bright. If the runners decide to fight, the Orks will battle until either half their number are down, or a runner unveils something to radically change the situation (a vehicle, an elemental, or other unusual item).

Archetypes

Orks: Use **Pedestrian (Ork),** p. 116, this book.

Info/Contacts

The Orks may have seen something or someone for which or for whom the runners have been searching. Even if they don't have anything now, they know the seamier side of the Sprawl *real* well.

At about three A.M., a loud pounding on the door rouses a runner from deep sleep. Grumbling and cursing, he draws his Predator, goes to the door, and opens it to find a large Ork staring him down.

Quotes

"Open da fraggin' door, chummer!"

"I'm Lou. Ya slottin' dweeb! Get outta here 'n get these folks in!"

"Whad'dya think happened! Some Humanis polis geeked my friends! These two're all that's left!"

Notes

The local Humanis Policlub's more radical members decided to make trouble tonight. While attending a huge rally march downtown, about 50 members drifted off and got into a firefight with some Orks. Most of the polis got wasted, as did eight of the ten Orks they attacked.

Lou is an Ork sorcerer who was out doing some heavy partying with friends. After the first bar ran out of booze, they went looking for another, and ran into the polis instead. Before Lou got a chance to start casting spells, the Orks were already in retreat.

Lou is protecting the last two Orks, and will make sure that the runner knows enough to keep the door locked until morning, by which time the polis will give up and leave. That's when Lou will head out to take on the last few polis. It should be a good fight. Of course, help would always be appreciated...

Archetypes

Lou: Use **Former Wage Mage** (Healer Orientation), p. 38, **SR** rules. Use Ork racial modifiers.

Polis: Use **Humanis Policlub Member**, P. 168, **SR**.

Info/Contacts

Lou is familiar with the Ork undergrounds and most of the places for buying fetishes at reasonable prices.

An Ork in an expensive suit approaches the runners. He is obviously a corporator, though an Ork higher-up is quite a rarity among the corps.

Quotes

"Evening, gentlemen. My name is Elliot Tanner, and I'd like to retain your services."

"I am having an unfortunate problem with discrimination, and I'd like you to help me."

"I know the usual prices and am willing to pay in the usual way."

Notes

Elliot Tanner is a mid-level supervisor at Fuchifax, the datafax greeting card firm. Virgil Burns, his superior, does not like Metahumans, and is deliberately blocking Elliot's deserved promotion. Elliot wants the runners to find some dirt he can use against Virgil to make him treat Metahumans better. It isn't blackmail for Elliot's own sake. No, he's a corporator and a gentleman. Elliot wants to help all Metahumans.

The places to find dirt on Virgil are many. His home computer, for example, could have some questionable financial records. If runners break into his condo, they would notice unusually expensive furnishings or possibly even some holopix of Virgil's Metahuman relatives.

Archetypes

Elliot: Use **Mr. Johnson**, p. 170, **SR** rules, without cyberware.

Virgil: Use **Company Man**, p. 164, **SR** rules. Add Ork racial modifiers.

Info/Contacts

Elliot knows many people in his business.

One of the runners is visiting a school-age sibling. As he and his kid brother/sister are leaving the building, he notices a crowd of kids pelting eggs at a well-dressed woman. Though it is not obvious at first, she is an Ork, probably the most beautiful the runner has ever seen.

Quotes

"Stop! This is—. Please!"

"People like you give all of us a bad name. Humans, Orks, Elves, Dwarfs, everyone."

"Whatever happened to all created equal? I teach people about that because I believed it was the truth."

Notes

Anna is an elementary school teacher. If she wanted to disguise herself, she could almost pass for Human. But she is an Ork who is proud of her racial origins.

Though constantly confronted with some form of prejudice, she tries to make others understand that she is a person, too. It's probably a losing battle, though.

Archetypes

Anna: Use **Street Doc**, p. 171, **SR** rules. Change Biotech to Teaching and Biological Sciences to History.

Info/Contacts

Anna knows many of the teachers in the city.

All day, runners have noticed Orks gathering together, muttering among themselves. As night approaches, Orks usually seen in the bars and other nightspots are absent. Like lemmings, all their kind are drifting in the same direction, toward one of the parks in the city. Standing alongside a heroic monument, an impressive Ork addresses the huge crowd.

Quotes

"We are all Orks! We must unite!"

"The Elves have a nation! The Dwarfs have a nation! The Humans have many nations!"

"Together we will march, and if they do not listen, then, *we will fight*!"

Notes

The Ork making the speech, Urtan the Bold, is famous among his people. Since he first emerged seven years ago, he has tried to help other Orks and to speak out in favor of an Ork nation. He calls for "one land, one people," and insists that,"Orks are people too." These slogans have won many to his thinking.

The Orks will listen to him speak for a good three hours, then march with him to the governor's mansion, where they will make their demands. Urtan will use the government's refusal to show that all Humans are Humanis at heart. After this confron-

tation, a night of rioting breaks out. All non-Orks hide in fear, waiting for the light of day.

Archetypes

Urtan the Bold: Use **Ork Mercenary**, p. 41, **SR**.

Typical Ork: Use **Pedestrian (Ork)**, p. 116, this book.

Info/Contacts

Urtan is a persuasive speaker. Orks (as well as members of other races) all over the globe pay attention to his words.

The runners receive a tip. Tonight a mob of gunmen will break into their samurai's apartment to blow him away. The tip is accurate, but someone forgot to mention that the gunmen would all be Orks.

Quotes

"Nuke da breeders! Fraggin' polis!"

"Drekkin' vat job. Slot 'is stick!"

"Geez, Tarry's right! The slottin' Humanis are here! Ever'one lock 'n load!"

Notes

It's a setup. Tarry, an Ork, is the head of security for a group of Ork diplomats. The six Orks with him are all bodyguards.

Tarry presented "evidence" that the runners were Humanis Policlub members intent on killing the diplomats. As head of security for the visit, it was easy for him to dispatch most of the other guards so that he could kill the diplomats himself. He's being paid by one corp to mess up Ork relations with a competitor.

Eventually, the runners will probably be able to make the Orks realize that they, the runners, are not Humanis, and have no intention of harming the diplomats. If the runners emphasize the fact that they were told that the Orks were mob enforcers and exactly when they would attack, the Orks will realize they've been betrayed. From there, it is a short step to the real traitor's identity.

Tarry plans to wipe out the diplomats by throwing a grenade into the hoverlimo's passenger compartment. If the runners (or the Orks) can figure out the plot, more power to them.

Archetypes

Tarry: Use **Ork Mercenary**, p. 41, **SR** rules.

Ork Guards: Use **Pedestrian (Ork)**, p. 116, this book.

Info/Contacts

The Ork guards have contacts with all manner of people in the Sprawl.

A mob of people swarms through the streets, most carrying guns. Such shouts as "Up with the common folk!" "Send the trogs and dandies back where they came from!" are heard.

Quotes

"Trolls and Orks are forcing real people out of jobs in security areas!"

"It's not safe for real people anymore 'cause of all the dandelion-eaters 'n Dwarfs."

"Let's put 'Grumpy' and 'Sleepy' back where they belong: two meters under."

Notes

The local Humanis Policlub has had enough. They're swarming like locusts through the streets, looking for Metahumans. Before the night is over, few people will think Humanis is just a bunch of cranks, and any Metahumans not hiding under their beds could well be burned alive.

There are over a hundred polis, and so straight firepower will not be effective in the long run. The best way to fight them is with words, if the runners can get their attention long enough to talk.

Archetypes

Poli: Use **Humanis Policlub Member**, p. 168, **SR**.

Info/Contacts

The Humanis Polis are people from every walk of life, from corps to vagrants, from deckers to samurai.

Eight men and women are walking down the street, wearing sickeningly sweet smiles. They're dressed similarly, too, in boots, blue corduroy pants, and white sweaters. They hand out pamphlets to everyone.

Quotes

"Good morning, friend."

"We're here to tell you about Brother Michael's New Life drive."

"We're building a better tomorrow today, a wave of cleanliness. We need help. Don't give money. Give of yourself."

Notes

The New Wave, Brother William Monroe's band of followers, have made a decision to clean up the Sprawl. All are out trying to enlist the help of those who have the biggest stake of all: the people living in the Sprawl.

They don't have influence. They don't have firepower. All they have is a sincere desire to set things right. If their movement gains strength, runners and other people who live by their own law may be forced out of this "brighter tomorrow."

The New Wave will probably gain some strength, but it's hard to tell how much influence they can attain. Though a corp that chooses to remain nameless does contribute some money to the group, the New Wave and its leader are sincere and honest.

Archetypes

Brother William: Use **Metahuman Rights Activist**, p. 169, **SR** rules.

Wave Member: Use **Humanis Policlub Member**, p. 168, **SR** rules.

Info/Contacts

As in any groundswell movement, people of every persuasion and profession are drawn to the New Wave.

The trid is broadcasting a meeting between the governor and a bunch of dandelion-eaters.

Quotes

"We do not deny that this is a growing city and needs space. We hope you will not deny us the same."

"But Governor, we do not seek to halt the Sprawl's expansion, merely to curb it."

"Look, frowsy, dumpy, and terminally unwashed, will you listen to what we're trying to say?"

Notes

A group of Elves are in town trying to lobby the city to cut back on expansion into the surrounding woodlands because it destroys so many Metahumans. In the Elven lands, Elves are beginning to fear the outbreak of some kind of "holy war." It is these Elves who hope to influence the city to avoid more misunderstandings and bad relations.

Many complications can arise. Some Humanis type might try to assassinate them. A Metahuman runner might decide to teach someone a lesson. That is not to mention the stubborn attitude of the governor. In any event, tempers will be running high.

Archetypes

Elven Ambassador: Use **Company Man**, p. 164, **SR** rules. No cyberware.

Bodyguards (3): Use **Elven Hitman**, p. 166, **SR**.

Info/Contacts

The Elves will talk to anyone willing to listen, but will avoid revealing how dissatisfied are many of their people.

A group of very loud Orks is marching down the street, singing songs and waving placards. Lone Star and Eagle patrolmen, street cops, and Humanis are gathering. It's beginning to look uncomfortably like a riot.

Quotes

(Sung in gravelly voice) "It's a small world after all. It's a small…"

"Orks are people, too!"

"Just 'cause we ain't Humanis, don' mean we don' need drekkin' water 'n heat!"

Notes

This Ork Policlub is doing its best to simulate a peaceful demonstration. One of them has dug up an old Disney song as a theme, others wrote placards, and they're on the march.

The Humanis took down signs announcing a government-sponsored meeting in the Ork part of the Sprawl. Because the Orks did not show up, water and heat allocation to the Ork zone has been halved.

Orks are among nature's most destructive elements, but this group wants to use the law instead of physical force. If no one listens, things could get messy, especially with the way certain Humanis are acting.

Not everyone walking with the Orks is an Ork, though. Candy Harper (Metahuman rights activist) and Kerry Taylor (the noted reporter) are there to cover the story and help restore the resources the Ork community needs.

Archetypes

Ork Leader: Use **Troll Bouncer**, p. 173, **SR** rules.

Ork Demonstrator: Use **Troll Bouncer**. Subtract 2 on all stats (minimum 1).

Candy Harper: Use **Metahuman Rights Activist**, p. 169, **SR** rules.

Kerry Taylor: Use **Former Wage Mage** (Healer Orientation), p. 38, **SR** rules.

Info/Contacts

Like any political group, Orks have organizations and an "old boys network." This provides a great opportunity to get a line in, or even a date with Candy.

The runner's group is racially well-integrated. There's an Elf decker, an Ork samurai, a Dwarf techno, and a Troll fixer (great for difficult negotiating sessions). When the Humanis declare the team the "Unnaturals of the Month," both sides decide to do something about it.

Quotes

"You are an example of unnatural and obscene behavior."

"How can Humans willingly consort with such trash?"

"If you will not do the honorable thing and kill yourselves, we will gladly do the honors."

Notes

Every month, the Humanis polis pick some group of people to persecute. This month it's runners. Any Metahuman runners are marked for extinction, otherwise known as "evolution in action."

Archetypes

Humanis Policlub Member: Use **Humanis Policlub Member**, p. 168, **SR** rules, for typical member. Humanis samurai, deckers, and so on also exist.

Info/Contacts

The Humanis have contacts into most walks of life, as do the Metahumans they persecute. Otherwise hostile or indifferent Metahumans might aid the runners if they know that the Humanis are after them.

The runner with the most magic has received a present from a mob-connected contact that almost smells of power. Just as he's about to open it, there's a knock on the door. When he opens, there are several people standing outside.

Quotes

"You have what was taken from our lands, the bones of our ancestors."

"Our sacred objects belong only to our people, and certainly must not remain in this city."

"You will give us the stolen relics, or we will blow you and this building off the map."

Notes

Four months ago, a raiding party managed to steal some major artifacts from one of the Native American graveyards. The Indians realized it and sent people out to retrieve the sacred items. Among these items were the revered bones of deceased Sovereign Tribal Council (STC) members.

Archetypes

Indian Leader: Use **Eagle Shaman**, p. 76, **SR** rules.

Tribal Warriors (4): Use **Tribesman**, p. 48, **SR** rules.

Hired Help: Use **Mercenary**, p. 40, **SR** rules.

Info/Contacts

The five Indians are part of a younger group who have vowed to retrieve the sacred objects from the unbelievers at any cost. If the runner returns the present to them, he will be treated as a worthy associate any time the Indians meet him in the future.

As the runners enter the local TipTopTech ware shop, a chime rings out the first few bars of "Taps". Surrealistic posters of horror shows cover the walls, and trid screens around the room show an ad for the latest low-budget simsense flick, "Blood of the Ninja XX". A middle-aged guy with a cheap hairpiece stands behind the counter, a knowing leer on his face.

Quotes

"Good afternoon, chummers! Anything you want, you can find here, if ya know what I mean."

"What are you in the mood for today?"

"Welcome to Weird Paul's Elusive Experience Emporium!"

Notes

This is the local sleaze dealer. Scattered among the conventional simsense chips and readers are others of another stripe. Weird Paul has run this place for 15 years, and has seen it all. He will indulge any fantasy, for a price. Determined to make a profit any way he can, he is a good person to avoid. In special circumstances, he might be a good man to know.

Archetypes

Weird Paul: Use **City Official**, p. 164, **SR** rules.

Info/Contacts

Weird Paul knows the home phone numbers for many major media personalities. He knew these people when they were just starting out.

Most people try to avoid Bytehead Barry, a local simsense dealer, because he's always promoting some get-rich-quick scheme. Laden down with electronic paraphernalia and strange lighting fixtures, Barry approaches one of the runners.

Quotes

"I've got an idea!"

"I want to do my own simsense series. The first one's called *Running the Night,* and you're the star!"

"I'm already lining up a decker for the next episode, *Cyberfish in the Net.* He's nuts about it."

Notes

Bytehead Barry's latest scheme is a beaut. He's decided to use the (illegal) equipment in his shop to duplicate and modify simsense chips to create his own simsense features.

It's a good idea, but Barry hasn't considered all the details. He wants to wire the runner's body to record simsense impressions, not realizing that this could have a negative impact on cyberware, and certainly would set off alarms in any normal security system the runner tried to penetrate. Nor does he realize that he hasn't the customary restraint circuits to prevent the chips from becoming BTL chips. Those are illegal, chummer,

and it's a crime to star in one.

Archetypes

Bytehead Barry: Use **Decker**, p. 34, **SR** rules. Change Computer (B/R) to Etiquette (Media).

Info/Contacts

BB knows other simsense dealers around town, and regularly checks in with the decker havens.

A runner's boyfriend decides to break it off with her, and then disappears. The only clue she can find in his apartment is a new simsense chip for the feature, *Do The Dead Really Sleep?*

Quotes

"Wow, a *real* simsense. Can I get a copy?"

"Wait a minute. This is way too real."

"Look at this waveform monitor. This chip violates the government regs on simsense highs. It's a BTL chip!"

Notes

Drew Productions, Ltd., the small company that produced DTDRS, ran out of money halfway through production. When a mysterious gentleman offered the two million necessary to complete DTDRS, the producers didn't read the fine print too carefully.

What it said was that Dr. David Smith, a noted psychologist working with the Yaks, would be using the feature to test a new technique for mass hypnosis. The hypnosis technique was added to about 250 simsense chips. The hypnotic instructions told the subject to immediately break off any intimate relationships, to send as much money as possible to Dr. Smith, and then to start thinking of himself as a zombie.

The runner's boyfriend is a victim of this conspiracy. When the runners realize what is going on, they can find the missing person in a graveyard. With him are about 50 other people who also believe they are dead, and that only by killing a living person can they return to life.

Archetypes

Dr. Smith: Use **Street Doc**, p. 171, **SR** rules. Add Psychotherapy 8.

"Zombie": Use **Pedestrian**, p. 116, this book.

Info/Contacts

Dr. Smith knows many other researchers in several related scientific fields.

A middle-aged man with a hairpiece that looks and smells like a dead skunk approaches the runners. His name is Weird Paul, and he has a business proposition.

Quotes

"I'm an honest businessman. I ain't got no trouble with you or anyone else. Why do people bother me?"

"I pay the gangs. I help you guys out when you need it. When will someone help *me*?"

"Look. These people, they're messin' in *my* biz, see? I need them erased, killed, neutralized. Unnerstand?"

Notes

Weird Paul of Weird Paul's Elusive Experience Emporium is usually a polite fellow. Now, however, a new competitor has been seriously denting his profits.

The new shop, Emerson Video Entertainments, is a small, clean store run by two recent immigrants to the Sprawl from some unknown country abroad. The store's whitewashed walls and tasteful displays are a pleasant alternative to Weird Paul's, which is plastered with horror posters and other grisly-looking props. Paul wants the runners to put this new shop out of business.

Archetypes

Weird Paul: Use **City Official**, p. 164, **SR** rules.

Francis Emerson: Use **Former Wage Mage** (Fighter Orientation), p. 38, **SR** rules.

Marilyn Emerson (his wife): Use **Merc**, p. 40, **SR**.

Info/Contacts

The Emersons are pleasant people who have already won the trust of most of the young folk in the Sprawl. Aside from their merchant skills, they keep up with current events in the corporate sphere.

The Swede, local shadowtech dealer extraordinaire, has obtained a black-market Attack Program that's supposed to be a marvel. He wants one of the runners to test it for him because the source who sold it to him is unfamiliar.

Quotes

"Chummer, would I do you wrong?"

"It's definitely Israeli, despite the casing."

"It's hardcoded ROM. Plug it in and it downloads itself partially into your deck, but the real wiz part stays locked in the cartridge."

Notes

The cartridge contains a powerful Attack program of a type never before seen on the street. That's because it was designed to meet a single customer's specifications.

The program is an Attack-12 that behaves normally the first three times it is used. On the fourth use, it lets loose an external Viral Construct (Attack 6) that turns and attacks the decker. The Viral Construct is unstable, lasting only four turns before breaking up. During that time, however, it can be damaged and/or destroyed like IC. If the decker attempts to run from it, the IC will pursue according to normal movement rules (1 node per action). Compute its initiative as an IC in a Red system.

Discovering the source, the intended destination of the cartridge, and how it got loose on the streets could become the basis for a major roleplaying adventure.

Archetypes

The Swede: Use **Fixer**, p. 166, **SR** rules.

Info/Contacts

The Viral Construct in the cartridge cannot be duplicated or copied by any player-character decker.

A runner has just picked up a hot new deck. The source may have been shady, but when did that ever matter? The deck works, it was cheap, and it's razor-edge tech. The only problem is that the deck is a hidden carrier-wave broadcaster that's got megapulse loads of corporate cops closing in for the kill. Seems the deck used to belong to a certain Matrix terrorist.

Quotes

"All right, Vermin, one move and you're ventilated!"

"Looks like that tracer chip worked after all."

"Who woulda thought the Vermin was actually a wimp like you."

Notes

The corps managed to bribe one of the Vermin's former associates to slip a broadcasting chip into his deck. Vermin, who knew his deck like the back of his hand, figured out what was going on real quick. First thing, he removed any electronic trace of his "friend" from the Grid, and then planted the chip in another deck and dumped it. The first time the deck is used, the chip will start to chirp and the corp cops will come running.

It will take some fast talk to convince the cops that the decker is not the Vermin, but it can be done. For one thing, the chip is not set up exactly the way the Judas inserted it into the deck. Additionally, the Persona is all wrong (no techno-bug here).

An interesting variation would be if the corps offered the decker the chance to prove his identity by finding the real Vermin.

Archetypes

Corp Cops: Use **Corporate Security Guard**, p. 165, **SR** rules, or **Company Man**, p. 164, **SR** rules, as needed.

Info/Contacts

Do well by the corps, and they just might have a job for a runner next time they need a freelancer.

ARCHETYPES & CONTACTS

This chapter includes eight new Archetypes and many new Contacts to supplement those provided in the basic **Shadowrun** rules. Archetypes are a starting point for player characters, but the statistics and descriptions can be modified if desired. A simple gender change does not require creating new statistics, but consult the Archetype Creation rules (page 53, **Shadowrun**) if planning to make more extensive modifications.

ARCHETYPES

BODYGUARD

"You blow it once in my line of work and you probably ain't never gonna work again. Who's gonna hire you if they know you blew it and a client got geeked? Reputation is everything.

"If you hire me, you can trust me. My eyes see everything, my ears hear everything, but I don't remember anything you want me to forget. That's part of my job. If you don't believe me, what's the point of me working for you?

"Hire me, and you can sleep easy. You're safe in my hands. Nobody gets near you, and if they try, I'll take care of them. I can play it as soft or hard as you want.

"I'll do anything you say, except when the drek starts to fly. That's when you do exactly as I say. If I say jump, you jump. If I say run, you run. When your life's in danger, it's my brawl game."

Commentary

The Bodyguard is a professional, and personal protection is his specialty. His job can be as boring as guarding a reclusive, house-bound computer programmer, or as exciting as protecting the latest sweet young simsense star during her first whirlwind tour of Europe.

Attributes
- Body: 6 (9)
- Quickness: 6
- Strength: 5
- Charisma: 3
- Intelligence: 5
- Willpower: 5
- Essence: .2
- Reaction: 5 (9)

Skills
- Car: 6
- Firearms: 6
- Negotiation: 4
- Stealth: 2
- Unarmed Combat: 6

Dice Pools
- Defense (Armed): 1
- Defense (Unarmed): 6
- Dodge: 6

Cyberware
- Air Filtration: 5
- Dermal Plating: 3
- Skillsofts
    - Armed Combat: 3
    - Bike: 3
    - Electronics: 3
    - Rotor: 3
    - Winged: 3
    - (4) Specialized Etiquette softs at 3 points each
- Skillwire: 3
- Smartgun Link
- Wired Reflexes: 2

Contacts
- Any Street, Corporate, or Media Type

Gear
- Colt Manhunter (with Smartgun Link, Firepower Ammo, Reactive Trigger, and extended clip)
- Ammunition (Heavy Pistol, 50 rounds, exploding)
    - Partial Heavy Armor
    - Armor Clothing
    - Tres Chic Clothing
    - High Lifestyle (2 months prepaid)

COMBAT MAGE

"No one argues that the samurai is lord of the physical street, but if you view that as the sum of existence, you are not long for this world.

"I am not the average mage. Though I'm interested in all matters arcane, my passion lies in the application of those mystical theories. My lifestyle is expensive, for I cherish all the finer things. One could not enjoy the life I do by pouring endlessly through myriad dusty tomes.

"I never worry about money, for my services are most useful to those who can pay me what I am worth."

Commentary

The Combat Mage is from that elite group of magicians dedicated to applying their magic martially. In a firefight, his sudden appearance can tip the balance. The Combat Mage is a lean, powerful fighting machine, and more than a match for most samurai. It would be foolish, however, for a Combat Mage to take on a samurai head-to-head. Guile and subterfuge will always be his most powerful tools.

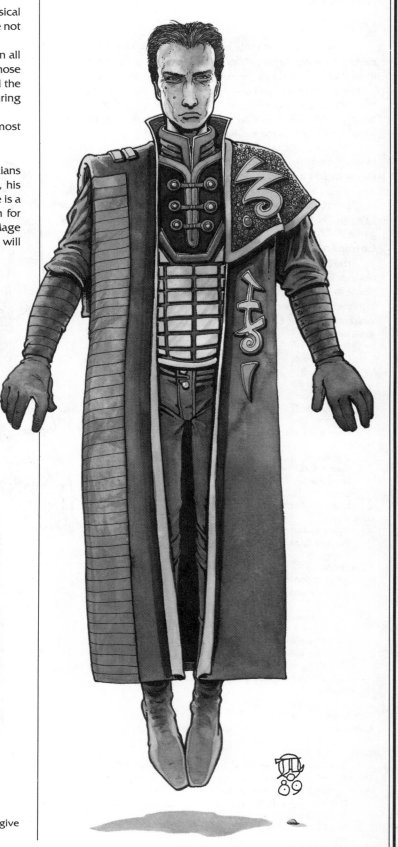

Attributes
Body: 2 (4)
Quickness: 4
Strength: 2
Charisma: 2
Intelligence: 5
Willpower: 5
Essence: 5.1
Magic: 5
Reaction: 4 (8)

Dice Pools
Defense (Armed): 1
Defense (Unarmed): 2
Dodge: 4

Cyberware
Boosted Reflexes: 1
Cybereyes (w/Thermographic and Low-Light)

Gear
Armor Jacket
Flash-paks (3)
HK227 SMG (w/ laser sight and 50 rounds)
Power Focus (1)
Spell Lock (Armor/2 successes)
Spell Lock (Personal Combat Sense/4 successes)

Skills
Conjuring: 3
Etiquette (Corp): 2
Firearms: 3
Magical Theory: 4
Sorcery: 6
Unarmed Combat: 2

Spells
Combat:
Manaball: 5
Mana Bolt: 5
Power Bolt: 5

Detection:
Clairvoyance: 5
Detect Enemies: 2
Detect Guns: 4
Personal Combat Sense: 5

Health:
Heal Moderate Wounds: 3
Increase Reaction: +2

Illusion:
Mask: 3

Manipulation:
Armor: 5
Confusion: 4

Contacts
Any Magic or Corporate Type

Notes
Don't forget that the Combat Mage's Boosted Reflexes (1) give him an additional +1D6 he receives to his Initiative.

DWARF MERCENARY

"Oh, har-har, I get it. That was a joke, right? I've got news for you, chummer. When I pull the trigger on my M22, I ain't gonna be the one knocked across the room.

"If it's been a hot spot, I've vacationed there. Got the tan and the scars to prove it. Wanna see my passport? Which one?

"You've got my last six personal efficiency reports in front of ya, with not a smudge of red ink on any of them. They're certified. If I'd doctored them, you'd know about it. Keep questioning my integrity, though, and they'll be covered in red.

"You know my rates. We got a deal or what?"

Commentary

The Dwarf Mercenary, though a rarity among the corporate armies of the world, is nonetheless a stalwart professional. His size has proven an advantage in rough terrain where a normal-size merc would become bogged down or hung up. Too many short jokes, however, and he'll hang you out to die.

Attributes
Body: 5
Quickness: 3
Strength: 4
Charisma: 2
Intelligence: 3
Willpower: 3
Essence: 5.5
Reaction: 3

Skills
Car: 4
Etiquette (Mercenary): 2
Firearms: 6
Gunnery: 5
Stealth: 4
Throwing: 4
Unarmed Combat: 5

Dice Pools
Defense (Armed): 1
Defense (Unarmed): 5
Dodge: 3

Cyberware
Boosted Reflexes: 1

Gear
Armor Clothing
Defensive Hand Grenades
FN-HAR Assault Rifle
    (100 rounds and
    laser sight)

Contacts
Bartender, Gang Member,
Merc, Rigger

Notes

ELF MAGE

"I am a student of the world and its laws. I do not refer to the laws of Man, but to the laws of the universe. Through my research and understanding, I have learned to bend those laws to my will. I speak now, and the universe leaps to my bidding. No, I did not think you would understand.

"Some seek to trivialize the great knowledge that is at our fingertips. I seek to further it. If what you request aids my own personal quest, then perhaps we can walk a while together.

"Do not mistake me. I am no ascetic. There is much we must still discuss regarding your debt to me…"

Commentary

More introspective than many of her magical compatriots, the Elf Mage should nonetheless not be disregarded as being purely cerebral, and therefore ineffective. Remember, too, that the she is still young.

Attributes

Body: 1
Quickness: 3
Strength: 1
Charisma: 2
Intelligence: 4
Willpower: 5
Essence: 6
Magic: 6
Reaction: 3

Skills

Conjuring: 4
Firearms: 2
Magical Theory: 5
Sorcery: 6
Throwing: 2

Dice Pools

Defense (Armed): 1
Defense (Unarmed): 1
Dodge: 3

Gear

Armor Jacket
Fetishes (Reusable for all spells she knows)
Flash Grenades (2)
Hardcopy Hermetic Library (2)
Lined Coat
Power Focus (1)
Ruger Super Warhawk (w/laser sight and 20 explosive rounds)

Spells

Combat:
Manaball: 4
Sleep: 7
Detection:
Clairvoyance: 2
Illusion:
Invisibility: 4
Manipulation:
Barrier: 3

Notes

Low-Light eyes. Check for Allergies. Low Lifestyle (2 months paid).

FORMER MAGE DETECTIVE

"Don't even bother trying, chummer. You can't lie in my presence. Hey, would *I* lie to *you*? Sure I got respect on the force. Who wouldn't, with my talents? Respect, but no nuyen. Comprende?

"So that's what you and me are going to talk about, 'cause there's no need to talk about anything else. You know who caught the Carlin Street Killer? Or who Old Man Sunnydale sent up the river? Wanna take a guess?

"For what you want, my talents and skills are perfect. Now, if your money is just as perfect, we just might have a deal. In fact, I know we do. How do I know? Trust me."

Commentary

A veteran of either a private or municipal police/security force, the Former Mage Detective is specifically geared to information-gathering and interpretation. When he heard the company was planning some cutbacks, including a freeze on pay, he walked and left a giant hole in his former employer's detecting capability. A hole he knows exactly how to exploit.

Attributes
Body: 3
Quickness: 3
Strength: 2
Charisma: 1
Intelligence: 5
Willpower: 5
Essence: 6
Magic: 6
Reaction: 3

Skills
Conjuring: 4
Etiquette (Law Enforcement): 2
Etiquette (Street): 3
Firearms: 3
Magical Theory: 4
Sorcery: 6
Unarmed Combat 2

Dice Pools
Defense (Armed): 1
Defense (Unarmed): 2
Dodge: 3

Gear
(3) Expendable Fetishes for all his spells
Armor Jacket
HK227 SMG (laser sight and 100 APDS rounds)
Micro-Transceiver
Power Focus (5)
Stimulant Patches (2)
Trauma Patches (2): 4

Spells
Combat:
Mana Bolt: 3
Ram: 5
Sleep: 4
Detection:
Analyze Truth: 6
Clairvoyance: 5
Combat Sense: 6
Detect Life: 6
Illusion:
Invisibility: 5
Manipulation:
Armor: 5
Control Action: 5

Notes
Middle Lifestyle

FORMER MILITARY OFFICER (LOW-GRADE)

"It makes me sick when I hear people bad-mouthing the government. They say we don't do anything, and that it's the corporations that really run things. Well, they don't know drek.

"Come on, let's unplug the simsense here, shall we? The only thing keeping the corporations in line is the government's military. Sure, they've got their 'corporate strike teams' and 'mobilized mercenary units', but we're everywhere. Do they have squadrons of stealth fighter/bombers? Nuclear carrier battle groups? Divisions of armor, infantry, and air cavalry?"

Commentary

The Former Military Officer still believes in a strong national military, even though current economics dictate the virtual impossibility of maintaining a full-size standing army. Nowadays, most national forces have been scaled down and specialized into small, elite units. With a locked command structure, upward mobility through the ranks is almost nil. Faced with this reality, the Former Military Officer, while maintaining his faith in the role of military, has begun to look elsewhere for his future.

Attributes

Body: 6
Quickness: 6
Strength: 4
Charisma: 3
Intelligence: 5
Willpower: 5
Essence: 5.1
Reaction: 5

Skills

Armed Combat: 2
Car: 2
Etiquette (Military): 4
Firearms: 5
Gunnery: 2
Leadership: 5
Military Theory: 4
Psychology: 1
Unarmed Combat: 5

Dice Pools

Defense (Armed): 2
Defense (Unarmed): 5
Dodge: 6

Cyberware

Datajack, 20Mp of Memory
Smartgun Link

Gear

Armor Jacket
Colt Manhunter (40 rounds Firepower Ammo, Smartgun Link, Reactive Trigger)
Doc Wagon™ Contract (Basic)
FN-HAR Assault Rifle (100 rounds, Smartgun Link, Gas-Vent (2) recoil reduction)
Helmet
Knife
Low-Light Goggles
Stimulant Patches (2): 5
Trauma Patches (2): 5

Contacts

Any Military, Mercenary, or Government type

FORMER TRIBAL WARRIOR

"What were you expecting, feathers and a war dance? Sorry if I've disappointed you, but we don't live in teepees, either. We've got cities, just like everyone else. The same cities, in fact, that the white man left behind when Howling Coyote showed them the truth. We have our own cities and our own land. It's my job to defend that land.

"Yes, our magic is powerful. But that's not all we rely on. We've got ridiculously oversized defense budgets, just like everybody else. With hundreds of kilometers of frontier to protect, we've invested in plenty of modern military hardware.

"So if you decide to sneak over our border some night, don't worry about desert spirits. Worry about our Raven attack helicopters."

Commentary

The Former Tribal Warrior was a regular soldier for one of the nearby tribal lands before he realized that border patrol and immigration supervision duty was not his true calling. Though he feels strongly for his homeland, he has gone outside the lands to satisfy his desire for action and adventure.

Attributes

    Body: 6
    Quickness: 6
    Strength: 6
    Charisma: 3
    Intelligence: 5
    Willpower: 4
    Essence: 5.3
    Reaction: 5

Dice Pools:

    Defense (Armed): 3
    Defense (Unarmed): 3
    Dodge: 6

Cyberware

    Low-Light Retinal Modification
    Smartgun Link

Contacts

    Any Tribal or Military type, or Fixer

Gear

    Armor Clothing
    Beretta Model 70 SMG (100 rounds,
     Gas-Vent (2) recoil reduction)
    Medkit
    Seco LD-120 (40 rounds)
    Simsense Player and 6 chips
    Survival Knife
    Thermographic Binoculars
    Trauma Patches (2): 4

Skills:

Armed Combat: 3	Etiquette (Tribal): 4
Athletics: 3	Firearms: 5
Car: 3	Gunnery: 5
Computer (B/R): 1	Rotor: 3
Electronics(B/R): 1	Unarmed Combat: 3

Notes

    Low Lifestyle

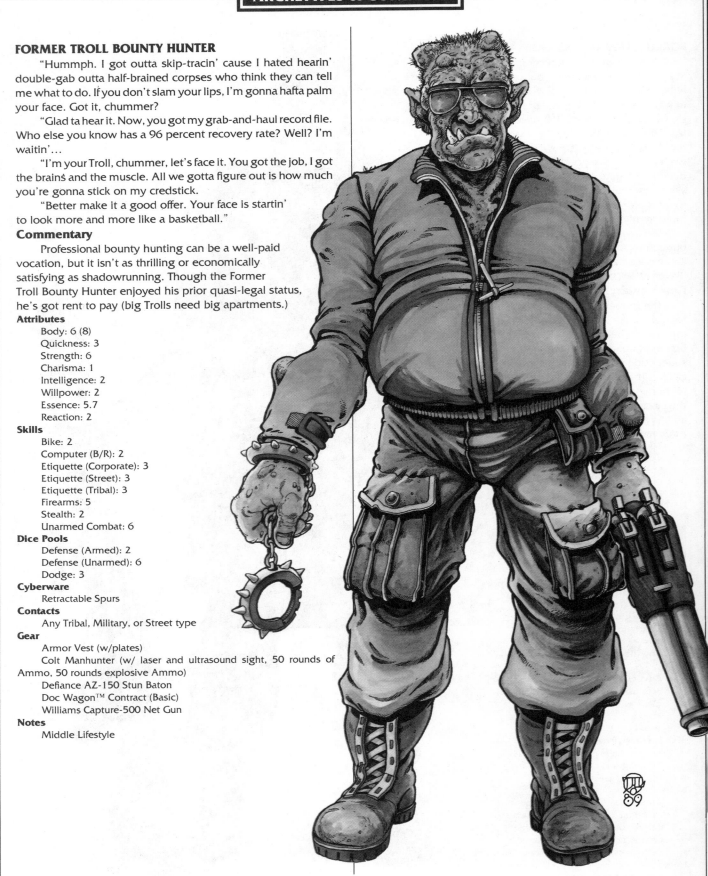

FORMER TROLL BOUNTY HUNTER

"Hummph. I got outta skip-tracin' cause I hated hearin' double-gab outta half-brained corpses who think they can tell me what to do. If you don't slam your lips, I'm gonna hafta palm your face. Got it, chummer?

"Glad ta hear it. Now, you got my grab-and-haul record file. Who else you know has a 96 percent recovery rate? Well? I'm waitin'…

"I'm your Troll, chummer, let's face it. You got the job, I got the brains and the muscle. All we gotta figure out is how much you're gonna stick on my credstick.

"Better make it a good offer. Your face is startin' to look more and more like a basketball."

Commentary

Professional bounty hunting can be a well-paid vocation, but it isn't as thrilling or economically satisfying as shadowrunning. Though the Former Troll Bounty Hunter enjoyed his prior quasi-legal status, he's got rent to pay (big Trolls need big apartments.)

Attributes
Body: 6 (8)
Quickness: 3
Strength: 6
Charisma: 1
Intelligence: 2
Willpower: 2
Essence: 5.7
Reaction: 2

Skills
Bike: 2
Computer (B/R): 2
Etiquette (Corporate): 3
Etiquette (Street): 3
Etiquette (Tribal): 3
Firearms: 5
Stealth: 2
Unarmed Combat: 6

Dice Pools
Defense (Armed): 2
Defense (Unarmed): 6
Dodge: 3

Cyberware
Retractable Spurs

Contacts
Any Tribal, Military, or Street type

Gear
Armor Vest (w/plates)
Colt Manhunter (w/ laser and ultrasound sight, 50 rounds of Ammo, 50 rounds explosive Ammo)
Defiance AZ-150 Stun Baton
Doc Wagon™ Contract (Basic)
Williams Capture-500 Net Gun

Notes
Middle Lifestyle

CONTACTS

Following are a number of new Contacts that do not appear in the **Shadowrun** basic rules.

ARMORER

"If it involves weaponry, it involves me. You need something tweaked, fudged, reinforced, upgraded, swapped, spiffied up, or just plain fixed, I'm your man."

Quotes

"Oh man, what did you do to this thing?"

"You will bring it back to me intact, won't you?"

Commentary

If it falls anywhere within the definition of "weapon," the armorer can tell you everything you ever wanted to know about it, and then some. He's your contact for any firearm, projectile weapon, personal weapon, or throwing weapon, regardless of how mundane or exotic.

Attributes

Body: 3
Quickness: 3
Strength: 4
Charisma: 4
Intelligence: 7
Willpower: 4
Essence: 4.7
Reaction: 5

Cyberware

Datajack, 100Mp of Memory
Retinal Display Link

Gear

Armor Clothing

Skills

Armed Combat (B/R): 5
Computer (B/R): 4
Computer: 4
Electronics (B/R): 3
Electronics: 4
Firearms (B/R): 6
Firearms: 3
Gunnery (B/R): 5
Projectiles (B/R): 4
Throwing (B/R): 3
Unarmed Combat: 2

CLUB HABITUÉ

"Wow, can you believe who's here tonight? I mean, we are discussing a major wizzer right here, tonight! This is the place to be, here and now. Wow!"

Quotes

"You're looking for a what kind of guy? Chummer, aren't we all?"

"I can't hear you. You're gonna hafta lean closer!"

"Hey, Mister, ya wanna dance?"

"Is that a gun in your pocket, or are you just happy to…Hey! That is a gun in your pocket!"

Commentary

The Club Habitué is on the hippest of the fast tracks. Just ask her, she'll tell you. The Club is her escape: wage slave by day, jazz girl by night. She thinks she knows everybody whose anybody, and might even tell you a thing or two about them, if offered her favorite drink.

Attributes

Body: 3
Quickness: 3
Strength: 2
Charisma: 4
Intelligence: 2
Willpower: 2
Essence: 6
Reaction: 2

Gear

Tres Chic Clothing

Skills

Unarmed Combat: 2

Special Skill

Club Rumormill: 2
Day Job Skill: 3

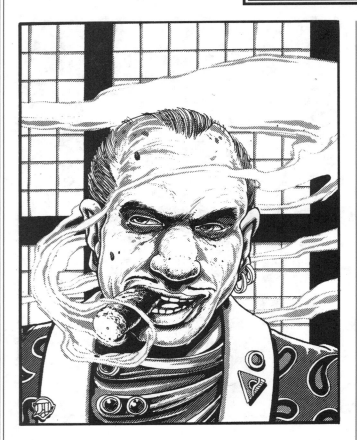

CLUB OWNER

"The joint's jumping tonight, ain't it? Warms my heart to see so many people having a good time. Dancing, drinking, laughing. I'm laughing, too. All the way to the bank."

Quotes

"Look, I don't care what you done someplace else. When you play my club, you're just another act and I expect to get what I paid for."

"Sure, I done a little biz with the Yaks. Everybody does. It's part of the cost of staying in business."

"Sure, I remember you, kid. What was your name?"

"Let's talk about this over lunch."

Commentary

The Club Owner is in this business strictly for the nuyen. Sharp and hard-nosed, he looks out for himself. He will help out his friends as long as he is sure he can keep his own skin clear of the trouble.

Attributes
Body: 2
Quickness: 2
Strength: 2
Charisma: 3
Intelligence: 3
Willpower: 3
Essence: 6
Reaction: 2

Skills
Etiquette (Media): 4
Etiquette (Street): 4
Negotiation: 4

Notes
Often accompanied by Bodyguard.

CORPORATE DECKER

"I don't care what some people say. I'm a company man and I love it. The corp's got the best hardware you've ever seen. It's hard to believe they actually pay me to use it. Even without that, I'd still be loyal to them. They really take care of you."

Quotes

"I just got this new (incomprehensible). It's great. Never seen anything this hot before."

"Look, I just work here. O.K.?"

"It's not my fault. The computer screwed it up."

"Must be a hardware problem."

Commentary

The Corporate Decker is another loyal employee of the corporation. He is happy with his lot, for he enjoys the limited hacking and mischief the corporation allows him to get away with in order to maintain his self-image. He works hard to keep his normally cushy job.

Attributes
Body: 2
Quickness: 3
Strength: 1
Charisma: 1
Intelligence: 4
Willpower: 3
Essence: 5.8
Reaction: 3

Cyberware
Datajack

Skills
Computer Theory: 4
Computer: 5
Etiquette (Corporate): 2

CORPORATE OFFICIAL

I'm a company woman, and damn proud of it. The corporation has done a lot of good things, not just for the metroplex, but for the country, even the world."

Quotes

"Good business is where you find it."

"No comment."

"I misspoke myself before. This is the real story."

Commentary

The Corporate Official is a cog in the machine of the corporation. She climbs the ladder of success with grim determination and vicious application of every skill she has. She is a shark who devours each bit of data that comes her way.

Attributes
Body: 2
Quickness: 2
Strength: 3
Charisma: 3
Intelligence: 5
Willpower: 4
Essence: 4.8
Reaction: 3

Skills
Etiquette (Corporate): 5
Interrogation: 4
Negotiation: 4

Cyberware
Datajack, 100Mp of Memory

CORPORATE RIGGER

"Take it from me, you ain't lived till you've screamed your rodded and rigged Nightsky across Federal Plaza at three in the morning, dodging rounds that would make those Express runners wet their panzers. Just me and the machine."

Quotes

"You want speed, I'm it. You want stealth, I'm it, too. You want both? Well, take a guess…"

"If you want the chopper on the ground at exactly 04:37:17, it'll be on the ground at 04:37:17. Guaranteed."

Commentary

Though he's still a company man, the Corporate Rigger retains much of the wild, hell-bent nature that makes him so good at this kind of work. Don't mistake his arrogance for a lack of experience, however. Nobody drives them better.

Attributes
Body: 4
Quickness: 6
Strength: 3
Charisma: 4
Intelligence: 6
Willpower: 4
Essence: 4.5
Reaction: 6 (8)

Skills
Car: 6
Computer: 3
Electronics: 3
Etiquette (Corporate): 4
Firearms: 3
Gunnery: 3
Rotor: 5

Cyberware
Cybereyes, Low-Light Thermographic and Flare Compensation
Datajack
Vehicle Control Rig (Level 1)

Gear
Appropriate Vehicle or Drones
Armor Jacket
Colt Manhunter

CORPORATE SCIENTIST

"The days of the independent research labs are gone. If you want to unlock the secrets of the universe, you have to punch a clock. I'm well-paid and can get what I need in the way of equipment and staff. Do I mind signing a lifetime work contract? No, not really."

Quotes

"They want to do what with my project? *No!* You can't let them…"

"Why wouldn't I be happy? I have everything. Everything."

Commentary

The Corporate Scientist is a hot commodity in intercorporate trade these days. The way they bounce from corporation to corporation keeps many shadowrunners in business. The majority are quite happy where they are, or else never reach the level of prominence where their expertise puts them in danger. Some don't even realize they've reached that level until that first mysterious stranger bumps into them.

Attributes	Skills
Body: 2	Appropriate Science Skill: 7
Quickness: 2	Computer: 4
Strength: 1	Etiquette (Corporate): 2
Charisma: 2	Related Science Skill: 6
Intelligence: 8	
Willpower: 5	
Essence:.7	
Reaction: 5	

Cyberware
Datajack, 500Mp International Memory
Retinal Display Link

Gear
Wrist Computer, 1,000Mp Memory

CORPORATE WAGE SLAVE

"I'm a company woman. We would all like to find an easy way out. I've tried. But now the corporation is my home and family. It's my life. What else can I do?"

Quotes

"Look, I just work here. O.K.?"

"You'll have to take that up with management."

"Excuse me, but I have to get back to work now."

Commentary

The Corporate Wage Slave is a loyal, industrious worker as long as she is under scrutiny. Even when nobody's looking, she is still unlikely to do anything that might endanger her soft position in the corporate structure. She has no real ambition beyond enjoying herself during her time off.

Attributes	Skills
Body: 2	Computer: 2
Quickness: 2	Etiquette (Corporate): 2
Strength: 2	**Special Skills:**
Charisma: 2	Being Ignored: 6
Intelligence: 2	Corporate Rumormill: 2
Willpower: 1	
Essence: 6	
Reaction: 2	

DER NACHTMACHEN POLICLUB MEMBER

"Nobody is going to tell us how to live, or how to die. It's for the people to decide. Not the corps. Not the government. And certainly not you!"

Quotes

"Down With Government! Down With The Megacorps! Down With Everything!"

"Live Free Or Die With Your Fist Up!"

Commentary

Born in the turbulent political breeding grounds of Divided Europe, Der Nachtmachen was one of the earliest policlubs to appear, and surprisingly, to register in North America. Until now, their numbers have remained relatively low, for their libertine anarchic philosophy had little appeal. Of late, however, their membership has begun to swell,.

Attributes

Body: 5
Quickness: 4
Strength: 3
Charisma: 2
Intelligence: 2
Willpower: 4
Essence: 6
Reaction: 3

Skills

Armed Combat: 5
Car: 3
Etiquette (Street): 3
Unarmed Combat: 4

Special Skills

Local Politics: 4
Rabble-Rousing: 3

Gear

Armor Vest
Car (Appropriately decorated with slogans)
Club
Spray Paint Can

Notes

Travels in pack of 1D6+1.

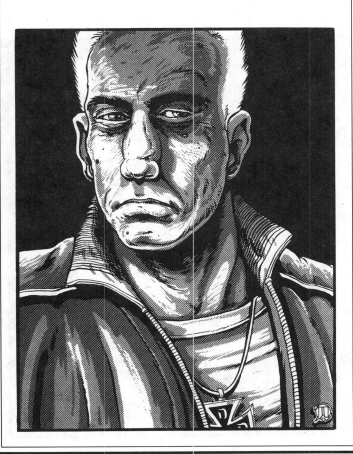

DOCK WORKER

"I work the docks, many times long after everybody else has gone back home to get some dinner and some sleep. Sure I see things. Doesn't everybody? I got a job, and a family of my own to think about, chummer. What's your offer?"

Quotes

"I wouldn't stand there if I were you..."

"Fish? Of course, I smell fish! Don't be an idiot."

"What ship did you say you was lookin' for?"

Commentary

With little to do besides lift and load, the Dock Worker always keep his eyes and ears open to what's going on around him. He probably knows a lot, but the docks are a tight-knit community. It's not easy to persuade him to betray that trust.

Attributes

Body: 6
Quickness: 3
Strength: 6
Charisma: 3
Intelligence: 3
Willpower: 4
Essence: 6
Reaction: 3

Skills

Athletics: 3
Car: 3
Etiquette (Corporate): 2
Negotiation: 2
Throwing: 3
Unarmed Combat: 3

Gear

Club

Notes

On the docks, at least 1D6 other Dock Workers are always present.

ELF POSER-GANG MEMBER

"Ain't you ever seen an Elf before? Of course, we're Elfs. It's cool to be an Elf. Cross us and you'll quickly learn how uncool it is to be dead. Samma wagga kan?"

Quotes

"I swear we're gonna become a chapter of the Ancients…someday."

"We Elves are the true powers in this town. You'd best not forget that, lest you suffer the consequences. Kan?"

Commentary

To be a member of an Elf Poser-Gang, one must be an Elf, or at least look like one. To that end, all members of the gang have undergone varying degrees of cosmetic surgery to give them that characteristic "Elf" appearance. Anyone who spends any time with members of a poser-gang will learn that they suffer almost uniformly from a serious inferiority complex, with a desperate need to appear as something better than they are.

Attributes	Skills
Body: 4	Bike: 3
Quickness: 4	Unarmed Combat: 2
Strength: 2	Armed Combat: 2
Charisma: 3	Firearms: 3
Intelligence: 2	**Special Skill**
Willpower: 2	"Elf" Gang Speak: 2
Essence: 6	
Reaction: 3	

Gear

Ares Crusader Machine Pistol (Two extra clips)
Armor Clothing
Honda Viking Motorcycle
Sword

FAN

You know that you're the best, don't you? Nobody else in your league. I've got all your best lines memorized. A friend of mine even set up pseudo-stims for me. I play 'em back all the time. Of course, it can't be anything like the real thing, but I suppose it's as close as I'll get to the thrills or the danger. What's it really like out there?

Quotes

"I can't believe that I'm really talking to you. This is real wiz!"

"I remember the time when you…"

"No! Hey, don"t run away!"

Commentary

The Fan may seem like a loser, the kind of person someone should avoid. Every fan has some talent, connection, capability, however, that just might be very useful in the right circumstances. Suffering a little hero worship is a small price to pay for the aid the Fan would give so freely.

Attributes	Skills
Body: 2	Etiquette (varies): 2
Quickness: 2	Other skill useful to his idol: 5
Strength: 2	**Special Skills**
Charisma: 1	History of Idol's Career: 8
Intelligence: 2	
Willpower: 1	
Essence: 5.5	
Reaction: 2	

Cyberware

Chipjack
Stimjack

FIRE FIGHTER

"You'd think the people of this city would understand. They live here, this is their home. Burn it down and you're only hurting yourself. I just don't understand sometimes."

Quotes

"Lady! Don't panic! We're coming up to get you!"

"Fires like this don't just happen. Somebody makes them happen."

"There's no water pressure. Somebody or something in the sewers must have ruptured a pipe. No, I don't know what we'll do."

Commentary

The Fire Fighter is an employee of one of the corporations contracted to do city-wide fire fighting. Like the Metroplex Guardsman, he desperately wants to make a difference. Everything, however, seems to work against him. Corporate bureaucracy, local political machinations, and underequipped and understaffed trucks all make his job harder than it needs to be.

Attributes

Body: 5
Quickness: 6
Strength: 5
Charisma: 3
Intelligence: 3
Willpower: 5
Essence: 6
Reaction: 4

Skills

Athletics: 3
Biotech: 3
Car: 2

Special Skill
Fire Fighting: 4

Gear

Fire Resistant Clothing (Armor Rating 0/1)
Micro-Transceiver Headset
Respirator

GOVERNMENT AGENT

"I'm always amazed at what these damn corporations think they can get away with. Don't they think anybody is watching? Well, I can tell you that *we're* watching."

Quotes

"Don't give me that corporate immunity drek. You're coming with me."

"Jurisdiction? There's no question of jurisdiction here. You've committed a federal offense."

Commentary

Holding a firm belief in the power and right of the government—be it the CAS, UCAS, Tribal, or Local—the Government Agent is nonetheless daunted and disheartened by the disdain the megacorporations show for his government.

Attributes

Body: 4
Quickness: 6
Strength: 4
Charisma: 4
Intelligence: 5
Willpower: 4
Essence: 2.8
Reaction: 5 (7)

Skills

Car: 3
Electronics: 3
Etiquette (Agency): 3
Etiquette (Political): 1
Firearms: 5
Interrogation: 3
Rotor: 2
Unarmed Combat: 4

Cyberware

Datajack, 50Mp of Memory
Smartgun Link
Wired Reflexes: 1

Gear

Micro-Transceiver
50,000¥ in appropriate electronic equipment

Notes

Never acts alone.

GOVERNMENT OFFICIAL

"It's a fact of life, son. The megacorporations all but own this country. Now, we can roll over and die, or we can fight them in ways they might not even expect. It's not going to happen over night, but it will happen. Meanwhile, we have to play their game, by their rules, and that might mean not always doing the right thing. But the ends justify the means, don't they?"

Quotes

"I'm sorry, but we have no comment at this time."

"We are taking it into committee, but I assure you that we will not let them get away with it."

"I disagree. The use of government forces in a situation like this is a completely improper allocation of those forces."

Commentary

The Government Official is a game player, be it the corporate or political game. He knows that sometimes he has to go along with something that doesn't sit right with him or that isn't beneficial in the short run. He has his eye on the long-term goal, however, and believes that attainment of that goal will justify his present actions.

Attributes

Body: 2
Quickness: 2
Strength: 2
Charisma: 6
Intelligence: 6
Willpower: 5
Essence: 5.6
Reaction: 4

Skills

Etiquette (Corporate): 6
Etiquette (Political): 6
Leadership: 4
Negotiation: 5

Special Skills

Economic Theory: 2
Politics: 4

Cyberware

Datajack, 20Mp of Memory

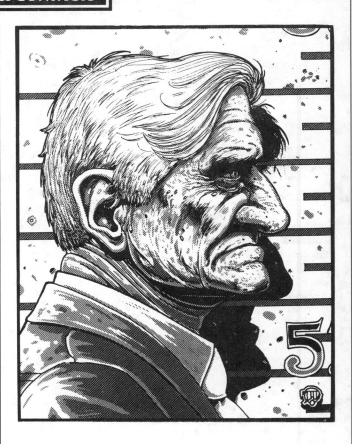

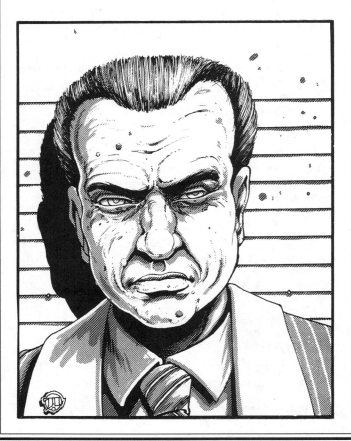

MAFIA DON

"It would behoove you to be more respectful to me. I control many things in this area, and that power could be used for or against you. If you understand how power works in this city, you will understand how unwise it is to trifle with me."

Quotes

"My people will listen to me. They know what will happen if they do not."

"Horses? I like horses."

Commentary

Heading a broad-based, multi-ethnic criminal organization, the Mafia Don is in a position that commands respect, and he knows it. The only time he will tolerate anything else is if the other party has the force to back it up.

Continuing the Mafia's long-standing traditions, the Don has sworn his people not to deal in BTL chips. Unfortunately, not all his lieutenants are obedient.

Attributes

Body: 2
Quickness: 2
Strength: 2
Charisma: 6
Intelligence: 7
Willpower: 6
Essence: 6
Reaction: 2

Skills

Etiquette (Family): 5
Interrogation: 3
Leadership: 6
Negotiation: 6

Special Skills

Local Politics: 4
Neighborhood Knowledge: 3

Notes

Always has at least 2 Mafia Soldiers with him.

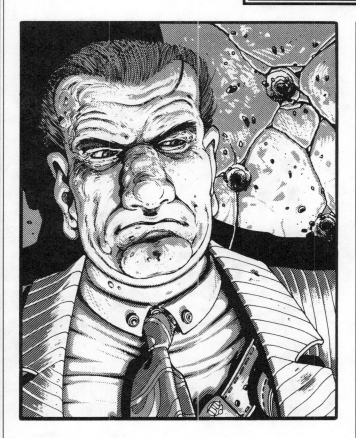

MAFIA SOLDIER

"You've got an attitude, punk, and it's one that's gonna get you geeked. If you're going to talk like that, you better move it outta here. *Now*. Why don't you try it on the Yaks and see how they like it? Yeah. Thought so."

Quotes

"The name's Janowitz. Why?"

"This is our territory, these are our people. The Don says if you mess with them, you mess with him."

"I think you should leave. We wouldn't want to stain the tablecloth."

Commentary

The Mafia Soldier is a loyal member of the family, doing the bidding of the Don and his lieutenants. Far from dumb or ignorant, the Soldier acts as a kind of "Block Captain," relaying information up and down the ladder of gang hierarchy. Sure he's tough, but so's his neighborhood. And when the Don calls, he'll be there.

Attributes

Body: 5
Quickness: 4
Strength: 4
Charisma: 3
Intelligence: 4
Willpower: 3
Essence: 5.3
Reaction: 4

Skills

Car: 3
Etiquette (Family): 4
Etiquette (Street): 5
Firearms: 5
Interrogation: 3
Unarmed Combat: 3

Special Skills:
Local Rumormill: 4

Gear

Ares Predator II
Armor Clothing

NEWSMAN/MEDIA ENTREPRENEUR

"Look, anybody can cover the news. You just point the camera and press 'record.' No big deal. What takes talent is setting it up so that the viewers think they're interested. We all know the public doesn't give a drek, but it's my job to help them pretend that they are."

"They have enquiring minds, and besides, it's their fundamental right to be informed. At least that's what we'll tell them."

Quotes

"Let me come along and cover it. I won't release till you give me the go-ahead. And I guarantee identification distortions for everybody on your team."

"Wizzer! That was great! But could you do it one more time, and, um, look a little *meaner* this time?"

Commentary

This archetype comes in two basic varieties: the network-affiliated or the independent newshound, and the entrepreneur. Both are in the broadcasting business and unless bought by a corporation, know that uncovering dirt is good for the ratings. The crowd still loves a good muckraking almost as much as spectacle.

Attributes

Body: 3
Quickness: 3
Strength: 2
Charisma: 6
Intelligence: 5
Willpower: 4
Essence: 6
Reaction: 4

Skills

Computer: 2
Etiquette (Corporate): 3
Etiquette (Media): 5
Etiquette (Street): 4
Etiquette (Tribal): 3
Negotiation: 4
Stealth: 3
Unarmed Combat: 2

METROPLEX GUARDSMAN

"I liked it better when we were the National Guard. People respected us more. But since the politicians got their way, we're the Metroplex Guard. We're supposed to be some kind of 'accommodation" with the S-S Council. Isn't the government still part of the UCAS? I suppose that it don't really matter. We still do the same jobs. I just wish we had the stuff the private armies play with. They've got some very heavy hardware."

Quotes

"It's our job to keep the peace. But if you want to make trouble, we can accommodate you there as well."

"What am I doing here? I could be home right now."

Commentary

As part of an emergency peace-keeping force, the Metroplex Guardsman is under the direct orders of the governor. Though under-manned and ill-supplied compared to corporate forces and professional security cops, the Guardsmen are citizens proud to serve.

Attributes

Body: 4
Quickness: 4
Strength: 4
Charisma: 2
Intelligence: 3
Willpower: 3
Essence: 6
Reaction: 3

Skills

Etiquette (Corporate): 2
Etiquette (Street): 2
Firearms: 5
Unarmed Combat: 4

ORK RIGHTS COMMITTEE MEMBER (ORC)

"You heard it right. O-R-C. It stands for the Ork Rights Committee. We're dedicated to seeing Orks get a fair shake in city politics. Think about it. How many Orks are sitting on the city council now, and how much of the population do we represent? You can see we've got a problem and who's even mentioned bigotry yet?"

Quotes

"Orks are people, too."

"Orks have the same rights as any other sentient."

"We'll take our cause to the streets if we have to."

Commentary

The ORC Policlub is dedicated to the protection of Ork rights, and they'll fight for those rights in the council chambers, in corporate corridors, or in the streets, if necessary. Though their political clout is strong, many ORC members have taken to "direct negotiation" with those who violate Ork rights, especially members of the Humanis Policlub (particularly those connected with Alamos 20,000).

Most ORC members are Orks, but a growing minority consists of enlightened Humans and other races.

Attributes

Body: 7
Quickness: 2
Strength: 6
Charisma: 2
Intelligence: 4
Willpower: 4
Essence: 6
Reaction: 3

Skills

Etiquette (Political): 3
Leadership: 2
Negotiation: 3
Sociology: 3
Unarmed Combat: 3

ORK SHAMAN

"Humph. You think the Powers of Nature do not call to us, too? Her Special Children? All of us hear, though few listen, and even fewer obey. That will change in time, as will the balance of all things. Such is the Wheel."

Quotes

"The Spirits Dance to my call, breeder."

"The wind howls tonight, my friend. Can you not hear its pitiful wail?"

"The ways of Man are not for us. Soon we will see the coming of the New Way."

Commentary

Sometime early in his life, the Ork Shaman was initiated into the Path of the True Way and he began his walk. Though he knows not where this road leads, he is sure it is the way that he and all the rest of his people must walk. He believes that the Great Mother has a special place for her Children, and awaits the revelation of that knowledge.

Attributes
- Body: 5
- Quickness: 2
- Strength: 5
- Charisma: 4
- Intelligence: 5
- Willpower: 6
- Essence: 6
- Magic: 6
- Reaction: 3

Skills
- Armed Combat: 3
- Conjuring: 6
- Magical Theory: 4
- Sorcery: 4
- Unarmed Combat: 3

Spells
- Any three with force levels totaling 15.

Gear
- Sword

PARAMEDIC

"Every time we go out there, I'm afraid of what I'm going to see. The worst is getting a call out to the middle of some hell-on-earth where some poor-slob BTL chiphead kid has decided he's a drek-brained shadowrunner. Sometimes I just don't understand what's going on here."

Quotes

"Lady! Stay there! We're coming up to get you!"

"Look, chummer, you just fell six stories and you've got at least a dozen bullets in you. I'm telling you, a stim patch just ain't gonna do it."

Commentary

The Paramedic sees it all. When people go off the deep end or when street action just gets too hot, he is often the one who comes in to tend to the casualties. From the tragic to the ridiculous, the paramedic knows the worst that can happen and the causes of it all, but he feels helpless to change things.

Attributes
- Body: 3
- Quickness: 4
- Strength: 3
- Charisma: 3
- Intelligence: 4
- Willpower: 3
- Essence: 6
- Reaction: 4

Skills
- Biotech: 5
- Car: 3
- Cybertechnology: 1
- Firearms: 2
- Unarmed Combat: 2

Cyberware
- Patches (5 of each kind)

Gear
- Armor Jacket
- Flash Grenade (1)
- Smoke Grenade (1)
- Medkit

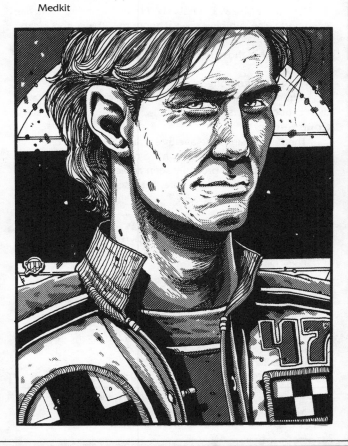

PEDESTRIAN

"Who me? Naw, I'm nobody. I'm just going to work like everybody else. Nothing special about me. Thank god."

Quotes

"Wow! Are those real cyberspurs you've got there? Can I see them?"

"ohgod ohgod ohgod ohgod ohgod…."

"Ummm…I ain't never seen a Troll before…and I certainly didn't shoot you…sir."

Commentary

The Pedestrian is the average citizen. He's part of the 99 percent of the population who have no cyberware, rarely see real magic, and have probably seen an actual dragon a grand total of twice in their lives. Sure, they see some of the other races, but doesn't everybody?

RACIAL MODIFIERS					
	Human	Elf	Dwarf	Ork	Troll
Attributes					
Body	3	3	4	6	8
Quickness	3	4	2	3	2
Strength	3	3	5	5	7
Charisma	3	5	3	2	1
Intelligence	3	3	3	2	1
Willpower	3	3	4	3	2
Essence	6	6	6	6	6
Reaction	3	3	2	2	1
Special Skills					
"Professional" Skill	3				

Gear
Normal Clothing

PLAIN CLOTHES COP

"I watch the streets. I see what goes on. I'm working to keep law and order as best I can, but it's tough. The uniformed guys usually have to jump in when something happens, but most times I need to hang back and see where it leads. We can't sweat the small stuff."

Quotes

"Metro police. Nobody move!"

"Look, buddy, I can help you. I'm a cop."

"Que hablo Colt Manhunter?"

Commentary

Be he from government-backed or corporate police, the Plain Clothes Cop knows the street better than anyone. He knows how to move with it, how to become part of it, or how to disappear for weeks at a time. He senses the street's ebb and flow so well that the hairs on the back of his neck prickle at the slightest change. He also understands that someone in his work can't always just come down hard. Sometimes he's just gotta play the game.

Attributes

Body: 4
Quickness: 5
Strength: 3
Charisma: 3
Intelligence: 4
Willpower: 5
Essence: 6
Reaction: 4

Skills
Car: 3
Etiquette (Law Enforcement): 4
Etiquette (Street): 7
Firearms: 5
Military Theory: 2
Psychology: 4
Sociology: 3
Unarmed Combat: 4

Gear
Colt Manhunter
Micro-Transceiver

REPORTER

"You've got a story to tell. I've got an ear to listen. Everybody's got something to hide, and it's my job to find out what it is. Hey, if it's not hiding, it's not worth finding."

Quotes

"You gotta let me in! The people have a right to know!"

"I'm sorry, but I can't reveal my sources. You understand."

"You say he was with *who*? Well, well…"

Commentary

With the dozens of datafaxes jamming the average person's electronic mailbox, the news-gathering business has become quite competitive. The ability to update an edition and transmit it within twenty minutes has made speed and secrecy blood-brothers in the reporting business. Help the reporter out, and he won't forget the favor.

Attributes
Body: 3
Quickness: 5
Strength: 2
Charisma: 5
Intelligence: 6
Willpower: 5
Essence: 4.3
Reaction: 5

Cyberware
Datajack, 100Mp of Memory
Display Link
Telephone

Gear
Armor Clothing
Dodge Scoot
30,000¥ of Surveillance Equipment

Skills
Car: 2
Etiquette (Corporate): 5
Etiquette (Political): 5
Etiquette (Street): 5
Firearms: 3
Interrogation: 6
Negotiation: 5
Unarmed Combat: 3

Special Skill
Nose for News: 5

SASQUATCH ENTERTAINER

(Uses Perkins-Athabaskan sign language for speech) "Wonderful sounds! Sing joyous! Cry high, dance low, I will make them for you now."

Quotes

"You have a wonderful voice. May I take it?"

"Diving-bombing starfighter with overloaded gravdrive and unstable fusion pack? No problem. How loud?"

"(Forest/bird noises) Isn't it beautiful? If we are not careful, my sounds are soon all we will have left of the forests."

Commentary

Declared a sentient species by United Nations decree in 2046, the Sasquatch has since begun a slow migration into more urban areas. While still rare, a Sasquatch Entertainer is a sight to behold. Grinning wildly, he enjoys his incredible ability to imitate sounds almost as much as running through the early morning forest. A Metahuman Rights Activist usually accompanies him as a translator.

Attributes
Body: 8
Quickness: 3
Strength: 7
Charisma: 3
Intelligence: 3
Willpower: 2
Essence: (6)
Magic: 6*
Reaction: 4

Skills
Unarmed Combat: 6

Special Skills
Sound Mimicry: 8

*Sasquatch are credited with shamanic magical capability, but few practice it.

The Sasquatch is a Dual Nature Being with a +1 Reach.

SIMSENSE STAR

"My agent says that I should be real careful about what I say. So I am, you know. My image, he says. It's real important.

Quotes

"Wiz! Real wiz!"

"You're so big and strong. Hey, you're like beautiful, you know."

"Like. It was like. Well. It was. Really."

Commentary

She/he is beautiful beyond your dreams, and her/his lifestyle comes out of those dreams. She/he is also property of the corporation. Look, even experience (simchips available at a reasonable price), but don't ever touch.

Attributes
- Body: 3
- Quickness: 3
- Strength: 3
- Charisma: 6
- Intelligence: 3
- Willpower: 4
- Essence: 4.7
- Reaction: 3

Skills
- Athletics: 4
- Bike: 3
- Car: 3
- Etiquette (Corporate): 4
- Media Etiquette: 6
- Negotiate: 6

Cyberware
- Custom simsense rig
- Senselink and internal transmitter

SNITCH

"Me? Why would I know anything? I tell ya, I just live round here. I don't hear nothin', I don't see nothin'. What's that? Thirty nuyen? We'll, ya know, I do kinda remember."

Quotes

"Geez, if they found out I talked to you, they'd have my scalp."

"Man, oh man, I shouldn't be tellin' you this, chummer, but…"

"Me? I ain't no snitch! I didn't tell you nothing! Right? RIGHT?"

Commentary

The Snitch may be the most weasely fellow ever born, but oh what he can tell you for a couple of nuyen. He's managed to stay alive this long, so maybe there's something to the old adage about God smiling on fools. Either that, or the Snitch is not as dumb as he looks.

The Snitch can be used as a "Street" Type for Contact purposes.

Attributes
- Body: 2
- Quickness: 6
- Strength: 2
- Charisma: 1
- Intelligence: 3
- Willpower: 2
- Essence: 6
- Reaction: 4

Skills
- Etiquette (Street): 4
- Negotiation: 4
- Unarmed Combat: 2

Special Skill
- Local Rumormill: 6

Gear
- Armor Vest
- Walther Palm Pistol

STORE OWNER

"This is my store, and I've lived in this neighborhood for 40 years. No matter what happens around here, this is where I'm staying. Business is O.K., and nobody bothers me too much. And I'll tell ya, them Orks down the block are fine by me. At least they pay their bills. Not like some others around here."

Quotes

"You wanna squeeze it, you buy it."

"Watch that pyramid of cans, kid. It took me hours to set up."

"…and that's how long it'll take you to put them back exactly the way they were!"

Commentary

Part of the neighborhood's eyes and ears, the Store Owner sees the same people day in and day out. He knows their routines and has a handle on their personalities. When somebody makes a change, it's as obvious to the Store Owner as if the person were suddenly wearing war paint. If a bunch of strangers suddenly appears in the neighborhood, he'll know it.

Attributes

Body: 4
Quickness: 2
Strength: 3
Charisma: 4
Intelligence: 3
Willpower: 5
Essence: 6
Reaction: 2

Skills

Firearms: 3
Negotiation: 5

Special Skill

Neighborhood Rumormill: 5

Notes

Remington Roomsweeper under the counter. Lone Star PANIC BUTTON within reach of his foot.

STREET KID

"Hey, chummer! Have I got something to tell you! Hey! Will you listen to me! I know what I'm talking about! It's that guy on the trideo, the one with the big grin. He's got a girlfriend in a condoplex. Oh sure, now your eyes light up."

Quotes

"Hey, mister! You the one who's looking for the Weasel?"

"Sure, I'll watch the place. How much is it worth to ya?"

"Look, I may be a kid, but I know all about that sort of thing. No, really, I do…"

Commentary

No matter where you look, there's the Street Kid, and she gets annoying really fast. Don't give her the quick, cool brush-off, however, because you can't tell who she might know or what she might have heard. Be careful, too, because in her eyes, you're *somebody*, more of a person than her parents ever were.

Attributes

Body: 2
Quickness: 6
Strength: 2
Charisma: 4
Intelligence: 4
Willpower: 3
Essence: 6
Reaction: 5

Skills

Armed Combat: 2
Athletics: 4
Etiquette (Street): 4
Stealth: 3
Unarmed Combat: 2

Special Skill

Street Rumormill

Gear

Armor Vest
Knife

Notes

3 out of 6 Street Kids have a pet dog.

TAXI DRIVER

"Sure chummer, I'll take you there, but it's gonna cost you extra. No, I ain't particularly worried about gettin' hurt. It's the car that takes a beating in the neighborhood."

Quotes

"Three hundred-fifty nuyen, chummer. Inflation, ya know."

"I got the back of this cab so armored, you could set off a nuke back there and I'd barely notice. You keep acting up and I'll just drive both of us over to the police station to say hello."

Commentary

The Taxi Driver is only trying to earn his piece of the pie. For a price, he'll take you just about anywhere you want to go, and for a different price, maybe even tell you about other passengers who have ridden in his cab. You need to know the hottest night spots or where the employees from a certain corp go for saki after work? Just ask, and he might even tell you.

Attributes	Skills
Body: 3	Car: 5
Quickness: 3	Etiquette (Street): 2
Strength: 3	Firearms: 3
Charisma: 4	Unarmed Combat: 2
Intelligence: 4	**Special Skill**
Willpower: 5	Street Rumormill: 3
Essence: 5.2	
Reaction: 3	

Cyberware

Datajack, 50Mp of Memory
Retinal display Link for local map

Gear

Armor Jacket
Browning Ultra-Power Ford American modified with extra Armor (1 pt) and a Thick Armor Glass partition inside.

TECHNICIAN

"Slow down. You're always in too much of a rush. Tell me again what the problem is. You tried the debug? Let me see that thing. Ease off. I know you said you tried it, but I just wanted to see for myself. Well, I think I have a good idea what the trouble is. Have it for you next Tuesday. You want it by when? That'll mean a rush charge. O.K., chummer, it's your credit."

Quotes

"Must be a software problem."

"You want quality. You have to pay for it."

"Don't rush me. This delicate stuff takes time."

"I could fix it for you if I had the parts."

"I can fix anything if the credit's there."

Commentary

The Technician is the man to see when hardware or an electronic device is not operating correctly. He may be a legitimate businessman, a corporate suit, or even a black marketeer. One way or another, he is a man of invaluable skill.

Attributes	Skills
Body: 2	Biotech: 3
Quickness: 3	Computer Theory: 5
Strength: 3	Computer: 4
Charisma: 2	Computer (B/R): 6
Intelligence: 6	Cybertechnology: 3
Willpower: 4	Electronics (B/R): 3
Essence: 5.8	Electronics: 3
Reaction: 4	

Cyberware

Datajack

TERRORIST

"My cause is just, and in time, you will see its righteousness. Few understand now, but that will change. My actions will one day brush the sleep from the eyes of a truly Awakened world."

Quotes

"There are no innocents."

"What must we do then? Allow these atrocities to continue? No. We must make the world listen."

Commentary

The Terrorist is a firm believer in his cause, be it that of a policlub, opposition to environmental destruction, or of an oppressed people. He believes terrorism is necessary because every other avenue has been exhausted. He targets either his opposition or something that can hurt them, but will not excuse anyone who stands on the sidelines.

Attributes	Skills
Body: 3	Armed Combat: 3
Quickness: 4	Car: 2
Strength: 3	Demolitions (B/R): 3
Charisma: 4	Demolitions: 3
Intelligence: 4	Firearms: 6
Willpower: 3	Psychology: 4
Essence: 3.5	Unarmed Combat: 4
Reaction: 4 (6)	

Cyberware

Smartgun Link
Wired Reflexes (1)

Gear

Ares Predator II (with Smartgun Link)
Armor Clothing
FN-HAR Assault Rifle (with Smartgun Link)

WIZ KID MAGE

"Hey-hey, the wiz ain't just for you olders. Gray-hair, let me tell you how it's done. You grab the Art by its neck, smack it into shape, and leave it whimpering to follow at your heel. None of this mumbo-drek. Just power."

Quotes

"Anybody up for a little wiz-bang?"

"Me? No, I ain't never lost it. Now, Jimmy over there….yeah, the one with the limp and twisted-joker grin. Now *he* lost it …"

Commentary

Mix the "Mr. Magic Home Training Simsense" with natural talent and a smattering of real magical training and you get the Wiz Kid Mage. Under-age for virtually everything, he nonetheless commands powerful magics. Often the Wiz Kids will group temporarily in Wizzer Gangs until the personality clashes result in a magical bloodbath of tragic proportions.

Attributes	Skills
Body: 2	Bike: 2
Quickness: 5	Conjuring: 2
Strength: 2	Firearms: 2
Charisma: 2	Magical Theory: 1
Intelligence: 3	Sorcery: 3
Willpower: 2	Unarmed Combat: 2
Essence: 6	
Magic: 3*	
Reaction: 4	

Spells

Combat:
Fireball: 3
Powerbolt: 4

Health:
Heal Moderate Wounds: 3

Illusion:
Chaos: 2
Mask: 2

Gear

Armor Vest
Fichetti Security 500
Suzuki Aurora

SPRAWL LAW

—The following is an abridgement from the data book *Modern North American Law,* by C.S. Windham, Modern Media (New York), 2050. Used with permission.

In the days of the lawless Old West, men claimed the right to walk the streets armed in the name of self defense. That right still holds in our own era, but severe limits have been imposed on what kind of firepower an individual can bring to bear in his own defense. Using an FN HAR assault rifle that fires armor-piercing, discarding-sabot ammunition against a knife-wielding ten-year-old is unacceptable and punishable by harsh penalties.

WEAPON RATINGS

Weapons are divided into categories that are rated with a letter code. Following is a list of weapons and their ratings.

SMALL BLADED WEAPON (A)
This includes all knives larger than a folding pocket knife with a blade under 18 centimeters, and impromptu sharp-edged hand-held weapons.

LARGE BLADED WEAPON (B)
This includes all swords, axes, polearms, and weapons with blades over 18 centimeters, including cyber hand razors and spurs.

BLUNT WEAPON (C)
This includes clubs, batons, and impromptu blunt-edged hand-held weapons.

PROJECTILE WEAPON (D)
This includes bows of all kinds and any weapon specifically designed for throwing.

PISTOL (E)
This includes all hold-out "light" and "heavy" pistols. Permits are 200 nuyen for possession and 500 nuyen for transport.

RIFLE (F)
This includes all sporting rifles and shotguns (both long- and short-barreled. Permits are 300 nuyen for possession and 600 nuyen for transport.

AUTOMATIC WEAPON (G)
This includes all submachine guns, machine pistols, and assault rifles.

HEAVY WEAPON (H)
This includes machine guns of all types, assault cannons, and other heavy-caliber weapons.

EXPLOSIVES (I)
This covers all types of explosives, including propelled or demolition charges.

MILITARY WEAPON (J)
This covers all military-grade/issued weapons not specified above.

PERMITS

Permits are available for possession and transport of certain weapons. In all instances, these permits are issued only if the applicant can justify the weapon's use in the home, to support courier purposes, or in other personal defense or job-related functions.

Special security permits are available for all the above-listed weapons, but are issued only to licensed security firms for use on company business by their employees. These permits are annual and cost 5,000 nuyen per category.

OTHER ITEMS

Though technically not weapons, certain other items have been grouped under that category for the sake of convenience.

Permits for these items are available from registered law enforcement/security personnel and agencies at 300 nuyen for an individual permit and 10,000 nuyen for an agency permit, per category, for one year.

MILITARY ARMOR (K)

This includes any heavy armor, either partial or full, intended for military, law enforcement, or security work.

AMMUNITION (L)

This includes flechette and exploding ammunition as well as armor-piercing discarding-sabot rounds designated as Military/Security rounds with restricted usage.

CYBERWARE

This category does not include hand razors and spurs, which are classified above. It is divided into Classes A, B, and C.

Class A (CA)

Smartgun Link or any weapon-targeting enhancement.

Class B (CB)

Any Reflex Enhancements or Vehicle Control Rigs, Muscle Enhancements, or Dermal Armor.

Class C (CC)

All cyberweapons and program carriers.

WEAPON OFFENSES

There are varying levels of weapons-related offenses covered by the law. These range from possession through deliberate use. They are listed below, with the numbers used to match the offense with the weapon group in the **Weapon Fines and Punishment** Table below.

POSSESSION (1)

Possession is simply that: owning or carrying the designated weapon.

TRANSPORT (2)

Transport is the act of carrying or transporting said weapon, either on one's person or in a vehicle.

THREAT (3)

Threat is the act of brandishing said weapon in public, whether or not the weapon was actively and intentionally used to threaten another. Carrying an externally visible weapon is considered a **Threat**.

USE (4)

This covers any usage of a weapon against or in the general vicinity of a living target or public or private property. It is not necessary to prove intent to harm for this offense, only usage. Neither must a harm have resulted from usage of the weapon.

WEAPON FINES AND PUNISHMENT TABLE

Weapon Type	1 Possession	2 Transport	3 Threat	4 Use	5 Intent
(A) Small Bladed Weapon	100¥	500¥	1,000¥	2,000¥/2 mths	5,000¥/6 mths
(B) Large Bladed Weapon	200¥	800¥	2,000¥	5,000¥/4 mths	10K¥/8 mths
(C) Blunt Weapon	150¥	650¥	1,500¥	3,000¥/3 mths	7,000¥/6 mths
(D) Projectile Weapon	300¥	1,000¥	2,000¥	3,000¥/4 mths	5,000¥/8 mths
(E) Pistol	500¥	1,500¥	5,000¥	10K¥/1 yr	2 yrs
(F) Rifle	1,000¥	3,000¥	8,000¥	18 mths	3 yrs
(G) Automatic Weapon	5,000¥	10K¥	6 mths	2 yrs	4 yrs
(H) Heavy Weapon	10K¥	20K¥	1 yr	4 yrs	10 yrs
(I) Explosives	10K¥	40K¥	1 yr	4 yrs	10 yrs
(J) Military Weapons	6 mths	1 yr	2 yrs	8 yrs	20 yrs
(K) Military Armor	1,200¥	—	—	—	—
(L) Ammunition	3,000¥	—	—	—	—
(CA) Class A Cyberware	5,000¥	—	—	—	—
(CB) Class B Cyberware	20K¥	—	—	—	—
(CC) Class C Cyberware	10 yrs	—	—	—	—

INTENT (5)

Intent is the same as for **Use**, except that said weapon is used explicitly to cause physical injury or property damage, whether or not such injury actually occurred. The effects of said weapon are dealt with under **Injury/Death Offenses,** below.

ENFORCEMENT

In official logs, Offenses are listed by their alphanumeric code. Thus, a Pistol (Possession) Offense would be listed as E1, and Automatic Weapon (Intent) would be G5. The punishments listed above are also the average maximum punishment, with great regional and situational variations.

Enforcement of weapons laws also varies according to the region and circumstance. Local law enforcement and security personnel have great discretionary power as to which laws to enforce and against whom. This has, of course, led to cries of discrimination and harassment from various policlubs or organizations. Also, local law enforcement organizations usually look the other way for certain circumstances or individuals who enjoy special favor with that law enforcement agency.

The local and neighborhood condition also affects which laws are enforced against whom. The worse the neighborhood, the more enforcement agencies focus on enforcing the more serious, higher-level offenses rather than the lower-level crimes. Neighborhoods have been unofficially rated according to their enforcement level. The following table indicates the average North American enforcement trends, based on neighborhood types. Actual enforcement practices do vary.

An "L" listing indicates Light Enforcement, with a low to almost negligible chance of the average pedestrian being stopped on the street by law enforcement personnel. "H" indicates Heavy Enforcement, with a high, almost certain, chance of the average pedestrian being stopped on the street. Note that the pedestrian's appearance affects his chances of being stopped, even in Light Enforcement zones.

The Security Rating of the neighborhood normally drops 1 level during late-night hours.

Note, too, that the "Z" Zone is an almost mythical region where no law enforcement personnel go. Circumstance may occasionally cause a "D" or "E" Zone to downgrade to a "Z", representing the local law enforcement agency's unwillingness to enter the area.

INJURY/DEATH OFFENSES

Rarely do Weapon Offenses stand alone, for usually an Injury/Death Offense is what brings about the Weapon Offense Charge. An Injury/Death Offense is an action that directly or indirectly results in the injury or death of another person. Following are general descriptions of the various types of Injury/Death Offenses.

Most offenses, unless otherwise noted, include the potential for parole after at least 30 percent of the prison term has been served. The offender will then remain on parole for another 20 percent of his prison term.

Note Injury/Death Offenses pertain equally to magic-induced injury or death.

ENFORCEMENT TABLE

Rating	Type	Enforcement
AAA	Business, Upper-Class Suburban, Upper-Class Downtown, Upper-Class Residential, Upper-Class	**H** (All Levels)
AA	Business, Upper-Middle Class Suburban, Upper-Middle Class Downtown, Upper-Middle Class Residential, Upper-Middle Class	**L**(A1, E1), **H** (all others)
A	Business, Middle Class Suburban, Middle Class Downtown Middle Class Residential Middle Class Industrial (Good Area)	**L** (A & E, 1-2)), **H** (all others)
B	Business, Lower-Middle Class Residential, Lower-Middle Class Industrial (Bad Area)	**L** (A-E, 1-2, & F1), **H** (all others)
C	Business, Poor Residential, Poor Industrial (Very Bad Area)	**L**(A-F, 1-3, & G1), **H** (all others)
D	Business, Very Poor Residential, Very Poor	**L** (A-F 1-3, G1, L1, CA 1), **H** (all others)
E	Business, Slum Residential, Slum Abandoned Zones	**L**
Z	Anarchy	**None**

RECKLESS ENDANGERMENT

An individual is charged with this offense only when, by sheer luck, no actual injury or death resulted from the action, whether or not the action was deliberate or accidental. The penalty is a fine ranging from 100 to 5,000 nuyen, depending on the severity of the endangerment.

ASSAULT

Assault is any action resulting in the injury of another person, whether or not that action was deliberate or accidental. The penalty for assault ranges from a 2,000 nuyen fine to 1 year in jail, depending on the severity of the assault.

MANSLAUGHTER

Manslaughter is any purely accidental action that results in the death of an individual. Manslaughter is often the charge of record when intent to kill is not provable. The penalty for manslaughter is normally 5 years in jail per offense.

MURDER

Murder is the charge when deliberate intent to kill is provable. The penalty ranges from ten years to life.

PREMEDITATED MURDER

This charge rarely occurs because it is often difficult to prove that the suspect planned and conspired to kill his victim. The penalty for premeditated murder ranges from 30 years to life with no possibility of parole:

ACCESSORY

Accessory is a supplementary charge to the above when the suspect is not involved in the physical action, but does contribute to its execution or planning. There is no accessory for either of the murder charges, only the charge itself. The penalty for accessory is roughly 20 percent of the base offense.

PROPERTY DAMAGE OFFENSES

Whenever property damage occurs as the result of an action, the normal course of law requires that the damage be recompensated at a rate based on a convicted offender's ability to pay.

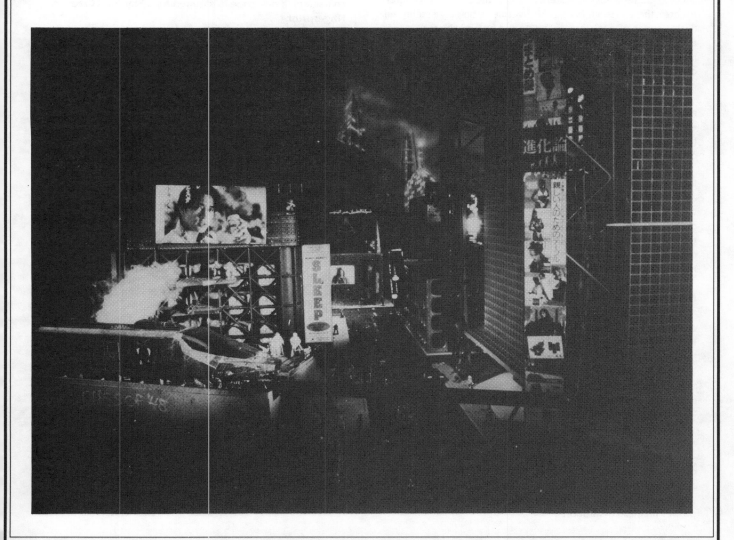

CREDSTICKS AND IDS

Someone once said that life revolves around the credstick. That may be an overstatement, but not by much. Most normal people *have* a credstick, but most shadowrunners *are* their credstick.

USING A CREDSTICK

In game system terms, the use of a credstick or ID verifier requires an Opposed Success Test, pitting the rating of the credstick/ID against the rating of the verification system. Both sides roll a number of dice equal to their respective ratings, using the opposition's rating as the Target Number. The side with most successes wins. If both sides win the same number of successes, the verifying system instructs the operator to "interrogate" the credstick bearer. The verifier's display screen will flash a series of questions based on the bearer's history, which the bearer must answer correctly. If he fails, the credstick or ID is rejected. This process requires a Negotiation Success Test, as described on page 153 of the **Shadowrun** rules. The verifier is automatically Suspicious of the bearer at this point.

Credsticks, in the **Shadowrun** world of 2050, are a combination credit card/ID card. A specially formed, high-density, encoded optical chip, the credstick serves as a credit card for financial transactions of all kinds. Physical currency is virtually obsolete, with the black market as a major exception.

Not only does the credstick contain an individual's System Identification Number (SIN) and his current financial balance, it also tells the verifying system, or the credstick checker, where to look to confirm the existence of these funds. As both the credstick and the financial institution holding these funds contain the verifying information, it makes forging a credstick very difficult. The detailed cross-referencing between the stick and institution will catch most forgeries.

FINANCIAL INFORMATION

Credsticks come in five levels, depending on the amount of funds they can access and the amount of cross-referencing information present. These levels are:

Standard Credstick 1 – 5,000¥
Silver Credstick 1 – 20,000¥
Gold Credstick 1 – 200,000¥
Platinum Credstick Up to 1,000,000¥
Ebony Credstick Virtually unlimited

To receive a certain level credstick, the bearer must have an account at above the maximum for the previous level credstick.

It is also possible to conduct transactions through direct connection between credsticks. Before the money becomes available, however, an electronic banking machine must be accessed and the information on the exchange forwarded to the proper financial institutions.

IDENTIFICATION LEVELS

As already stated, credsticks also serve as a form of identification. Differing levels of identification verification can be encoded onto the stick. To verify identification on certain types of credsticks requires special levels of ID verification:

Level 1 Passcode
Level 2 Fingerprint
Level 3 Voiceprint
Level 4 Retinal Scan
Level 5 Cellular Scan

Passcode

A simple alphanumeric passcode consisting of up to 30 characters, a passcode is required for a Standard Credstick.

Fingerprint

A thumbprint is required for ID confirmation. The stick holds a copy of the print and it is compared with the print on file at the financial institution. Silver Credsticks require both a Passcode and a Fingerprint.

Voiceprint

A Gold credstick requires a simple voiceprint as well as the Fingerprint and Passcode. The voiceprint is often taken passively through a pickup microphone in the credstick checker's area. No specific "voiceprint statement" is necessary, though verification requires at least three full sentences.

Retinal Scan

A detailed scan is made of the bearer's retinal pattern and compared with one on file at the financial institution. For redundancy, Passcodes, and Voiceprints are required for usage of a Platinum Credstick.

Cellular Scan

The bearer of an Ebony credstick may also have to pass a cellular scan as well as the Retinal Scan, Voice Print, and Passcode checks. The scanning process requires only a small cellular sample, such as a bit of skin.

OPENING AN ACCOUNT

When someone opens an account, the financial institution requires that individual to provide his SIN and to supply whatever Passcode, Fingerprint, Voiceprint, Retinal Print, or Cellular Print information appropriate to the level of credstick issued.

A person may have multiple credsticks representing multiple accounts at different financial institutions. He may, alternatively, have all the account records encoded onto one credstick for convenience.

Most financial institutions also make available a special form of credstick known as a certified credstick. Like cash or a bearer bond, the certified credstick is worth the amount encoded, with no identity verification needed. The issuing financial institution is, thus, encoding the stick with raw funds, money that exists nowhere else but on that stick. Use of a certified credstick is not limited to the individual for whom it was originally issued. Most financial institutions charge a small fee to create a certified stick, usually in the range of 2 to 5 percent. The certified credstick cannot be used for ID purposes.

All institutions that accept credsticks have credstick checkers to verify the existence of the appropriate account and the identity of the owner. The transaction will always be confirmed if a credstick is legitimate and the bearer is using his official SIN with correct ID, and all the passcodes and prints match. If however, even a small amount of the transaction or ID verification involves a forgery, game tests are necessary to determine whether the forgery is good enough to beat the system.

FORGING CREDSTICKS AND IDs

Forging a credstick is a difficult task. Though it may be easy enough to rig, it is identification that is difficult to replicate.

To verify a credstick ID, the information is cross-referenced and double-verified through a dozen or more channels. Such cross-referencing is a simple matter in the international computer Grid, and so it is the falsification of identity that requires an incredible amount of electronic effort. That is, someone must create and covertly insert into the world's data banks a suitable, appropriate, and credible "back history" that appears to have always been there.

No individual can accomplish such a task. Shadowy organizations exist solely for the purpose of creating false identities and false credsticks. These organizations, normally based out of any of the world's data havens, are accessible only through secret channels. Among the rare individuals who know how to get in touch with a forgery organization is a fixer, whether independent or corporate.

To create the back history and the forged stick itself costs money. The greater the detail and reliability of the back history, the higher the rating of the stick, and the more money it costs to produce.

Stick Rating	Cost
1 – 4	Rating x 2,000¥
5 – 8	Rating x 10,000¥
9 – 12	Rating x 50,000¥
13+	Rating x 250,000¥

At least half this money must be paid to the Fixer in advance. The stick will be ready in 2D6 hours, but the time can be reduced by 50 percent for double the cost.

Once created, the stick is, for all intents and purposes, real. Under most circumstances, it will withstand the verification process and be accepted.

It is only when particularly sophisticated credstick checking and ID verification systems are involved that a problem might occur.

VERIFICATION RATINGS

All credstick checking and ID verifying systems are rated by how efficiently they comb the world's data banks to verify the ID on the stick. The more efficient the cross-referencing, the higher the rating, and the longer it takes.

Rating 1

Rating 1 is the most basic credstick checker. Able to accept only a Passcode for ID verification, this rating is normally used by the average store or restaurant, places where use of an illegal credstick is rare and individual purchases unlikely to exceed 5,000¥. The verification process is instantaneous.

Rating 1 units can be portable and cost 12,000¥.

Rating 2 – 3

The Rating 2 or 3 system is more advanced. It can accept both passcode and fingerprint identification. Rating 2 or 3 systems are used where transactions in excess of 20,000¥ are unlikely. The verification process is instantaneous. Security and law-enforcement vehicles for on-the-spot ID checks also carry these rating systems. Some of the systems are portable, but most are linked to the local computer Grid. Installed Rating 2 or 3 units cost 45,000¥ and portable units 60,000¥.

Rating 4 – 5

Rating 4 or 5 credstick/ID verifiers can accept passcode, fingerprint, and voiceprint identification. They are used where transactions of more than 200,000¥ are unlikely. The verification process takes 1D6 minutes.

Rating 4 or 5 systems are also used in corporate or private security and law enforcement offices for detailed ID checks. These systems require local computer Grid access. They are available only from special sources, and range in price from 100,000 to 200,000¥.

RATING 6-7

Sophisticated systems, these ID/credstick verifiers are normally used for transactions in excess of 200,000¥, and additionally, as ID verifiers extraneous to financial transactions. These systems can accept Passcode, Fingerprint, Voiceprint, Retinal, and Cellular Print identification. The verification process takes 2D6 minutes.

These systems are also used by elite corporate and private security firms and by corporate "information" agencies. Government law-enforcement and intelligence agencies also use them. Occasionally, a Rating 6 or 7 system turns up in the possession of a wealthy or well-connected private individual. These systems require local computer Grid access.

Rating 8 – 9

Rating 8 or 9 systems are used for transactions in the 1,000,000¥ range and for sophisticated ID verification. Used only in the highest reaches of megacorporate and governmental pyramids, these systems are notorious for breaking all but the most solid of false IDs. They can accept all forms of ID verification. The verification process takes 3D6 minutes. Local computer Grid access is necessary.

Rating 10+

Some argue that these legendary systems do not even exist because of the enormity of the task of processing the vast amount of data-manipulation and cross-checking necessary to conduct so thorough a search. No other particulars are known about Rating 10 systems, whose existence is indicated only through rumor.

STREET SAMURAI CATALOG

A SHADOWRUN SOURCEBOOK

ON SALE NOW!

Dreamchipper

A SHADOWRUN ADVENTURE

ON SALE NOW!